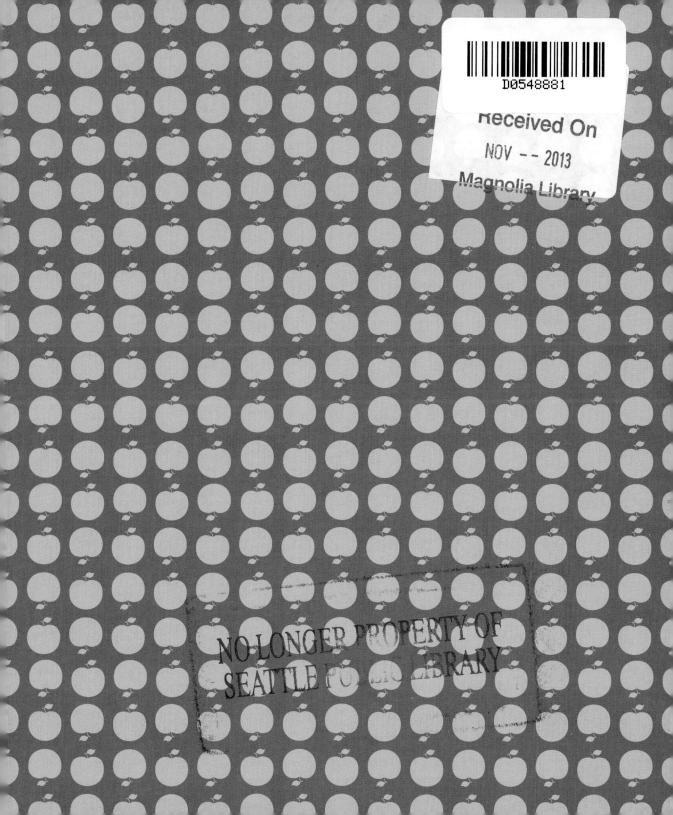

apples

FROM **HARVEST** TO **TABLE**

apples

FROM **HARVEST** TO **TABLE**

*50 recipes plus lore, crafts and more
starring the tried-and-true favorite*

Amy Pennington

Photography by Olivia Brent

St. Martin's Griffin
New York

table of contents

introduction

When I first starting telling people I was working on a cookbook dedicated to apples, the most common response was joyful exuberance. My sister immediately offered to share the recipe for her "famous" Christmas breakfast of apple-baked French toast. Plenty of others either offered suggestions or put in requests. What became quickly apparent is that everyone loves apples.

Apples come into season anywhere from summer to late fall, making them the quintessential season identifier for fall, though they keep nearly year-round in cold storage. Almost everyone, however, associates apples with crisp and sunny fall afternoons that require sweaters, smell of earth, and are filled with bright autumnal leaves. Every fall apples are harvested and binned in large wooden crates, further romanticizing this fruit—even stacked in a field in crudely stamped boxes, they are undeniably gorgeous.

There are thousands of cultivars of apples. The trees originated in Asia and were then brought to Europe. Our European ancestors brought the trees to America, where today we are the world's second largest global producer of apples with over half our supply coming out of Washington State. Apples are grown for variety of uses—fresh eating, cooking, and cider production among them. New cultivars are being created all the time, but older apple varieties, often referred to as heirlooms, tend to have greater variance in shape, color, and flavor. Typically, they are not produced in large quantities, because they are less either resistant to disease or do not produce as prolifically as a commercial variety does.

This means that apple availability varies from state to state. Some may have only the most popular varieties to choose from—Red Delicious, Granny Smith, and Gala among them. Thankfully, with a bevy of online farmers and specialty companies that ship, almost anyone can have any apple they please.

In the kitchen, apples can easily span across meals, and should. Cherished for their juicy sweetness, many varieties hold up equally well in savory dishes. They pair with typical fall flavors such as squash and sage, and can be eaten raw, roasted, shaved, dried, and sautéed with excellent results. Sweet apple dishes are easy to imagine, and there are far more ways to enjoy them than just traditional apple pie, which I have to admit I'm often too lazy to make.

I'm preferential to heirloom varieties, having grown up in New York with apple orchards close by and now living in Washington State where apple varieties are constantly being developed. East Coast and West Coast varieties differ, but both are nonetheless appealing—each offers something exciting. Be sure to check out the East Versus West sidebar on page 37.

For me, a perfect fresh and raw apple has a balance of sweetness and acidity in addition to a crispy bite. I like thicker apple skins that make you chew—the extra fiber is super healthy, and the sweet flesh is the reward. You may prefer juicier apples—those that leave juice running down your chin, and they do exist in perfectly ripe Honeycrisps. Eating apples are best used in salads and any recipe calling for a fresh apple.

As for baking apples, there are many to choose from, each with its own unique characteristics. When you select a baking apple, it's best to consider what you are hoping for in the final result. Some apples cook quickly to a fine pulp, like the pink-hued Winesap. Granny Smiths, on the other hand, will hold their shape when cooked, making them a nice choice if you're baking pie or want a cooked apple with a bit of structure.

It would take too much time to try to memorize what apples are best for particular recipes, so instead I suggest that you let your taste buds be the guide. Try to take advantage of fall harvest by eating apples as often as you can. Over time, you'll develop your own selection process and pinpoint your favorites. I like Spitzenburg, Liberty, Winesap, and Pippin the best.

I created these recipes in the hope of covering all of your apple bases. I include traditional recipes, like apple pie, along with nontraditional meals such as the Savory Barley-Stuffed Apples. Trying to break from the norm, there are a handful of recipes that come together easily and yet offer new and exciting flavor profiles. One of my favorites is apple slices tossed in lime and honey, served alongside a sugared ginger muesli. Try it—you'll love it! All recipes call for unpeeled apples, unless otherwise noted, for an extra boost of fiber and color. I have apples as meals and apples as snacks, and I even included a selection of apple crafts for kids. It's nice to keep little hands busy while you're in the kitchen cooking.

Now howd'ya like them apples?

breakfast & brunch

caramelized apples with vanilla crepes

Serves 6

Crepes are very much like pancakes in their preparation, though they are made in paper-thin disks that are folded before serving. These crepes are leavened with a small bit of beer, which also gives them an earthy and complex flavor that complements the syrupy caramel apples. Apples are caramelized in the oven here, freeing up stovetop space for crepe making. Cider or juice bakes down to a syrup, scented with ground cinnamon.

SUGGESTED VARIETIES: *Choose apple-y apples, like Golden Delicious, Rome, or Granny Smith.*

CREPES

2 cups milk

¼ teaspoon salt

½ teaspoon sugar

¼ cup (½ stick) unsalted butter, melted, plus more for pan and serving

1 tablespoon vegetable oil

1¼ cups all-purpose flour

3 large eggs

½ cup lager beer

1 whole vanilla bean pod, split, seeds reserved

APPLES

3 medium apples, peeled, cored, and cut into ½-inch wedges

1 tablespoon sugar

¼ teaspoon ground cinnamon

⅛ teaspoon salt

½ cup apple cider or juice

To prepare the crepes: In a medium mixing bowl, combine the milk, salt, sugar, melted butter, and oil. Set aside.

In another medium mixing bowl, add the flour and make a well in the center. Add the eggs and beat until incorporated. The batter will be quite thick and stiff. Slowly stir in the milk mixture, incorporating fully before adding more. Whisk in the beer and vanilla seeds. Set aside to thicken, 30 minutes to 1 hour.

To prepare the apples: While the batter is thickening, make the apples. Preheat the oven to 450 degrees F. In a large, shallow baking dish, combine the apples, sugar, cinnamon, and salt, tossing until the apples are evenly coated. Spread out the apples in single layer, being sure not to crowd or overlap them.

Bake for 10 minutes, until the apples are starting to soften, then remove the pan from the oven and stir well, turning the apples. Return the pan to the oven and bake until the apples are browning, about 5 minutes more. Now add the cider to the pan and stir to combine. Bake until the cider turns syrupy, about 5 minutes more. Remove the pan from the oven and set aside until you're ready to use it.

After the batter has sat (at least 30 mintues), set a small frying pan over medium-high heat until it's very hot. A drop of water splashed in the pan should sizzle and evaporate upon touch. Add a small spoon of butter (about ¼ teaspoon) to the pan and wipe out the excess with a paper towel, working to coat all sides of the pan. Ladle a small amount of batter into the pan, about ⅛ cup. Lift the pan slightly, swirling to evenly coat it with a very thin layer of batter. When the crepe is lightly browned, use an offset spatula or small kitchen spatula to flip it over. Cook the second side until it's lightly brown, about 1 minute.

Continue working in this fashion until all the crepes are cooked, stacking them on a plate. To serve, fold 2 or 3 crepes into quarters and fan them out on a plate. Spoon over a portion of the apples and serve immediately.

HEIRLOOM APPLES

Heirloom apples are growing in popularity, though there is ambiguity over exactly what an heirloom variety is. Before the onset of modern agriculture, produce was grown on a smaller scale, allowing for a wide diversity of plants. As the scope of agricultural business changed over the years, plants were selected based on their productivity, health, and consistency, narrowing down the options made available to the consumer.

The definition of what constitutes an heirloom plant is much debated, and there is no formal governing body to make the ultimate distinction. For the most part, heirloom plants are those that have been produced via open pollination (or, in the case of apples, grafting); they are often older plant varieties that are no longer available commercially. It is also worth a mention that no genetically modified organisms may be labeled as heirloom.

Heirloom apple trees tend to be regionally popular, as climates vary across the United States. Heirlooms are also unique in that they are often cultivated by small producers, allowing them to adapt to their particular environment over time, building up resistance to disease. Not all apple trees will work well in similar environments. A tree that flourishes in Washington State may not do well in upstate New York.

Sadly, many apple varieties are now thought to be extinct. Fortunately, many heirloom varieties can be purchased at local farmers' markets. These apples tend to have a wider diversity of seasonality, flavor, and texture than many commercial apple varieties.

Following is a short list of heirloom apple varieties available in national markets today: **SPITZENBURG, CORTLAND, MACOUN, COX'S ORANGE PIPPIN, NEWTOWN PIPPIN, NORTHERN SPY, IDARED, ARKANSAS BLACK.**

apple-stuffed french toast

Serves 4

This French toast is incredibly indulgent but comes together quickly. It's worth the caloric splurge! Layers of sweetened gooey apples are paired with cream cheese for the ultimate guilty pleasure. Make sure to let the French toast bundle sit in the egg wash, which guarantees a custardy bite.

SUGGESTED VARIETIES: *Choose apples that stand up to heat, like Golden Delicious, Rome, or Sonata.*

½ cup (about 4 ounces) cream cheese

2 tablespoons crushed pecans

¼ cup powdered sugar

4 large eggs

¼ cup milk

½ teaspoon ground cinnamon, divided

¼ teaspoon ground nutmeg

1 tablespoon vanilla extract

2 tablespoons unsalted butter, plus more for pan

2 medium apples, cored and sliced into thin slivers

¼ cup granulated sugar

½ loaf sliced white bread

Maple syrup, for serving

In a small bowl, combine the cream cheese, pecans, and powdered sugar. Fold together until well combined and set aside.

In a wide, shallow bowl, combine the eggs, milk, ¼ teaspoon of the cinnamon, the nutmeg, and the vanilla. Beat until the eggs are broken up and all of the ingredients are well combined. Set aside.

In a medium sauté pan, add 2 tablespoons of the butter and set over medium-high heat. Add the apple slices and cook until they are just beginning to soften, about 5 minutes. Add the granulated sugar and the remaining ¼ teaspoon cinnamon, and sauté until the apples are beginning to brown and the sugar turns syrupy, another 5 minutes. Turn off the heat and set the pan aside.

To prepare the French toast, lay out 1 slice of bread and spread with about 2 tablespoons of the cream cheese mixture. Mound a spoonful of the apples in the center, and cover with another slice of bread. Using the tines of a fork, crimp together the edges of the bread, sealing in the apples and cream cheese.

Transfer the stuffed bread to the egg custard bowl and let it soak for about 1 minute. Flip it over and let the second side sit and absorb the custard, about another minute.

Put a medium sauté pan over medium heat and add a bit of butter. When the butter is melted and warm, add the soaked and stuffed bread. Leave it to brown lightly, until it's golden brown, about 4 minutes. Turn the bread over and brown the other side, another 3 minutes. Remove from the heat and serve immediately, alongside the maple syrup.

potato pancakes with applesauce

Serves 4

These potato pancakes are crisp patties of grated potato seasoned with onion and fried to a perfect golden brown. They are best served with a dollop of sour cream and a generous spoonful of homemade applesauce. While potato pancakes are considered a traditional Jewish food, called latkes, they are a recipe fit for breakfast any day, especially when coupled with eggs. These pancakes also make a healthy and satisfying after-school snack for school-aged children. My nieces and nephews love them and are old enough to make the applesauce on their own while I grate, then fry, the potato pancakes.

SUGGESTED VARIETIES: *Cooking apples are best in this recipe, as they retain their apple flavor and easily break down to a smooth puree. Try Winesap, McIntosh, or Braeburn.*

APPLESAUCE

3 medium apples, cored and chopped into 1-inch dice	1 cup apple cider or water
	¼ cup sugar

POTATO PANCAKES

1 pound russet potatoes, peeled	3 tablespoons all-purpose flour
1 medium onion, grated on largest side of box grater	¼ cup sparkling water
	1 to 2 cups vegetable oil
3 green onions, top 3 inches of green trimmed off, finely chopped	½ teaspoon salt
	¼ teaspoon freshly ground pepper
2 large eggs, beaten	Sour cream, for serving

To prepare the applesauce: Add the apple, apple cider, and sugar to a medium saucepan and set it over medium-high heat. Once the mixture is boiling, reduce the heat to low and continue cooking, stirring occasionally, until the apples are soft and easily mashed with the back of a fork, 20 to 30 minutes. Pour into a blender and mix until all the apples are mashed and create a smooth puree. For a chunkier sauce with large bits of apples, mash by hand with a masher or the back of a large fork. Put into a small bowl and set aside to cool.

To prepare the potato pancakes: While the applesauce is cooking, grate the potatoes into a large mixing bowl, using the largest side of a box grater. Cover the grated potatoes completely with water and allow them to soak for about 15 minutes. While the

potatoes are soaking, add the grated onion, green onions, eggs, flour, and sparking water to another large bowl. Stir to combine, breaking up any clumps of flour. Set aside.

Preheat the oven to 200 degrees F.

To strain the potatoes, set a fine-mesh strainer over a large bowl and line it with cheese-cloth or a thin linen towel. Using a slotted spoon, transfer the potatoes from the water to the strainer, reserving the water. When all of the potatoes are transferred, squeeze out the cheesecloth or towel to remove excess water. Let all of the collected water sit for 10 minutes, so that starch collects in the bottom of the bowl. Then slowly pour the water off the potato starch, reserving the white paste.

Add the potatoes to the onion mixture and stir to combine. Add the potato starch and combine well.

Add 1 inch of vegetable oil to a large sauté pan, and set over medium-high heat. Using a large spoon, drop in 3-inch-wide rounds of batter, being sure not to overcrowd the pan. Cook until golden brown, about 4 minutes. Turn the potato pancakes over and cook the other side until golden brown, another 3 to 4 minutes. Remove from the oil with a slotted spoon and place on a layer of paper towels or a paper bag to drain. Once they've drained, place them on a platter and hold them in the warmed oven. Continue cooking in this fashion until all of the pancakes are done. Season with salt and pepper. Serve a platter of potato pancakes alongside a bowl of applesauce and sour cream, if using.

homemade apple sausage

Makes 8 sausage patties; serves 4

This sausage skips the casing and is loosely formed into a patty. Lean ground turkey is used as the main component and peppered with fresh sage and apples for added flavor. This sausage mix can be made ahead and held in the fridge until you're ready to use it. Feel free to add more herbs and spices to taste—this recipe is flexible and delicious.

SUGGESTED VARIETIES: *Select firm apples that retain their shape when cooked. Try Sonata, Cortland, or Granny Smith.*

---

1 pound ground turkey	1 teaspoon salt
10 sage leaves, finely chopped	1 teaspoon freshly ground pepper
1 apple, cored and finely chopped	2 tablespoons olive oil
1 tablespoon maple syrup	1 tablespoon unsalted butter

In a medium bowl, combine all of the ingredients except the oil and butter. Mix with your hands until well combined. Using a large spoon, scoop up some sausage mixture and shape it into a small hamburger-like patty. Continue forming patties in this fashion until the mixture is used up, about 8 patties in total.

In a large sauté pan, add the olive oil and butter, and set over medium heat. When the butter is fully melted, add the patties to the pan, being careful not to overcrowd. Cook until golden brown on one side, about 5 minutes. Flip the sausage patties and continue cooking until the second side is golden brown, another 3 to 4 minutes.
Serve immediately.

apple pancakes

Serves 4

Pancakes are a traditional American breakfast, but here we break tradition and opt for fiber-rich whole grains. These pancakes are also incidentally gluten-free for anyone with a wheat allergy or low tolerance to gluten. Grains are soaked overnight and then blended to a thin, smooth batter before being fried into a slender stack of hotcakes. These can be made ahead and frozen; simply pop one into a toaster for a quick and nutritious breakfast.

SUGGESTED VARIETIES: *A strong-flavored apple is important for these pancakes. Try Idared, Honeycrisp, or Macoun.*

½ cup steel-cut oats

½ cup quinoa, rinsed until water runs clear

½ cup applesauce

½ cup plain yogurt

½ cup water

1 teaspoon sugar

⅛ teaspoon salt

½ teaspoon ground cinnamon

½ teaspoon freshly ground nutmeg

3 large eggs

1 teaspoon baking powder

2 tablespoons unsalted butter, melted, plus more for pan and serving

1 small apple, finely diced (about 1 cup)

Maple syrup, for serving

Put the oats, quinoa, applesauce, yogurt, and water in a blender. Mix and cover, placing in the fridge overnight to soak. In the morning, add the, sugar, salt, spices, eggs, baking powder, and melted butter; blend on low speed to incorporate, at least 1 minute.

Move the setting to puree or liquefy and blend for 1 to 2 minutes more, until the batter is smooth and there are no big lumps.

Preheat the oven to 200 degrees F.

Place a large sauté pan over medium heat and add a pat of butter to the pan. When the butter is melted and the pan is hot, pour in batter by the ¼ cup, making as many pancakes you can without overcrowding the pan. Cook for 3 to 4 minutes, until the pancakes are golden brown and bubbles on the surface form and begin to pop. Flip the pancakes and cook the other side for another 3 to 4 minutes, until brown and cooked through.

Remove the pancakes from the pan and set aside on a plate; transfer to the warm oven until all the pancakes are cooked. Serve immediately, with syrup and butter if desired. Any leftover pancakes can be stacked and stored in the freezer in a plastic bag; place a piece of parchment between them to prevent sticking.

CIDER APPLES

Cider was a very popular beverage when settlers first arrived in America from Europe, a tradition brought over from England and other countries. Cider was often made in order to preserve the harvest—fermenting apple juice extends its shelf life.

Today, cider apples are different from traditional eating apples in that they are cultivated for cider production. *Cider*, in this instance, refers to the low-alcohol beverage known as hard cider. Hard cider is made by fermenting apples and converting their sugars to alcohol, which is very similar to the process for making apple cider vinegar (see p. 116).

Cider apples are categorized by their flavor components. Sweetness, acidity, and tannins are all weighted when making cider, resulting in a sorting system with cider apples labeled as sweet, sharp, bittersweet, or bittersharp. Most hard ciders are made with a combination of fruits, pulling from each of the flavor profiles. And while "sweets" are fine to eat, those considered "bittersweets" are off-putting due to their high tannin level and are guaranteed to make any mouth pucker.

Cider apples tend to be unsightly. They are hard, knobby fruits that are a far cry from the shiny smooth red apple more commonly available to consumers. Cider tree apple varieties are not sold commercially, and so the names of the apples will not sound familiar to most. Still, there are occasions when eating apples are used in cider. These come from orchard apples that will not make the grade to sell commercially. Since only fruits that look pretty are sold to consumers, small, blemished apples are sold at rock-bottom prices and used for apple juice and other products. For hard-cider makers, using this damaged fruit allows farmers to sell their ugly apples and charge a premium for the cider, thereby increasing a farm's profit margin. A win for all.

Some farmers are beginning to bring fresh cider apples to market—keep your eye out for these! Cider apples make excellent cider vinegar apples, and some of the sweeter varieties can complement apple butter or pies.

Popular cider apples: **GOLDEN RUSSET, GRAHAM SPY, BRAMLEY'S SEEDLING, ROYAL JERSEY, REINE DE POMMES.**

sweet potato, thyme & apple hash with egg baskets

Serves 4

Sweet potatoes are fried up into crispy cubes and paired with thyme-scented apples. Just before the hash is done, little "baskets" are made in the pan, and eggs are dropped in to cook alongside the vegetables. It is a perfect morning dish to get the day going—a well-balanced meal that is as healthy as it is delicious.

SUGGESTED VARIETIES: *Select firm apples that retain their shape when sautéed. Try Pippin, Cortland, or Granny Smith.*

---

3 tablespoons olive oil

2 tablespoons unsalted butter

½ medium yellow onion, finely diced

½ teaspoon salt

¼ teaspoon freshly ground pepper

1 medium sweet potato (about ½ pound), peeled and cut into medium dice

1 large apple, cored and cut into medium dice

4 teaspoons chopped fresh thyme (from about 10 sprigs)

4 large eggs

In a large sauté pan, heat the olive oil and butter over medium-high heat. When the butter is melted and beginning to fizz, add the onion, salt, and pepper and cook until it's just beginning to soften, 3 to 4 minutes. Add the diced sweet potato to the pan. Without stirring, cook the sweet potato until the first side is just browned, about 4 minutes. Toss and stir well, redistributing, and cook for another 2 minutes without stirring. Add the apple to the pan and cook, stirring often, until it's just softening and is warmed through. By adding ingredients to the pan slowly, you'll get sweet and nicely caramelized onion, crispy sweet potato, and just-cooked apple that will still maintain its shape and texture.

Reduce the heat to medium-low and make four 2-inch-wide wells in the sauté pan. To do this, push the vegetables aside with a spoon. Make sure the pan still has a bit of grease (add some butter to each well, if needed), crack 1 egg into each well, and cover the sauté pan. After 2 minutes, remove the lid and stir the sweet potato and apple without disturbing the eggs. Replace the lid and cook until the eggs are done to your liking: another 2 minutes (for an "easy" yolk), or up to 6 minutes (for a "hard" yolk). Serve immediately alongside toast.

apple-caraway soda bread

Makes one 9-inch round

Several years ago, I went on a daytime snowshoeing adventure with my chef friend Lynda. As an afternoon snack, she pulled a loaf of Irish soda bread out of her backpack, along with a sharp cheddar cheese and apples. It was delicious and hearty and quickly became one of my favorite quick breads to make. Here, I combine apple pieces in the dough before baking, creating a fruity mouthful with each bite. This bread is lovely toasted in the morning or served alongside cheese for a pre-dinner nosh.

SUGGESTED VARIETIES: *Try cooking apples that are tart but hold their shape, like Gravenstein, Jonathan, or Empire.*

---

2 cups all-purpose flour

3 tablespoons sugar, divided

1 teaspoon caraway seeds

½ teaspoon salt

1 teaspoon baking powder

½ teaspoon baking soda

3 tablespoons unsalted butter, chilled and cut into small cubes

1 small apple, finely chopped (about 1 cup)

¼ cup raisins

¾ cup buttermilk

1 large egg

Preheat the oven to 350 degrees F. Butter a baking sheet and set aside.

In a large bowl, combine the flour, 2 tablespoons of the sugar, the caraway seeds, salt, baking powder, and baking soda. Stir to combine.

Add the cold butter to the dry ingredients. Using your fingertips, cut it in until small crumbs form and most of the butter is incorporated. (You may also use the tines of a fork, if you don't want to use your fingertips.) Small clumps will still be visible. Stir in the chopped apple and raisins.

In a small bowl, whisk together the buttermilk and egg. Add the wet ingredients to the dry ingredients and stir to combine well, making sure all of the flour is completely incorporated. The dough will look and feel like a thick batter and be pretty wet, sticking to your fingers when handled.

Scoop or pour the dough onto the center of the baking sheet, shaping it into a small dome. Sprinkle remaining tablespoon of sugar evenly over the top of the dough. Bake immediately, for 30 to 35 minutes, until the bread is golden brown and a knife inserted into the center comes out clean. Let cool before serving. This bread will keep for several days at room temperature and lightly wrapped with parchment paper.

BAKED APPLE CHIPS

Baked apple chips are perfect for after-school snacking and a great way to get kids involved in their nutrition. Thin slices of apples are sweetened slightly then slow-baked to crisp, tasty slivers. Make apple crisps in large quantities, storing any extras in an airtight bag in the fridge, which will discourage molding from any natural lingering moisture.

Makes 5 cups

1 teaspoon vegetable oil

1 cup water

1 cup sugar

1 teaspoon ground cinnamon

4 medium apples

Preheat the oven to 175 degrees F or its lowest setting. Line two baking sheets with parchment paper, coat with a few drops of vegetable oil, and spread to coat the paper. Set aside.

In a medium saucepan, add the water, sugar, and cinnamon; set over medium heat. Stir constantly until the sugar is just dissolved, about 5 minutes, and remove from the heat to cool.

To prepare the apples, use a mandoline or knife to slice them about ¼ inch thick. Don't worry about coring or seeding your apples—all will bake up to an edible chip. Add the apple slices to the syrup in the saucepan, and let them marinate for 30 minutes.

Drain the apple slices from the syrup and place on the baking sheet, being sure not to overcrowd the pan. Bake until the apples are dry and their edges are just beginning to crisp, 2 to 3 hours. Remove the pan from the oven and leave the apples on it to cool completely.

When the apples are thoroughly cooled, store in an airtight container or plastic bag until you're ready to use them. Apple chips may be stored in the fridge or moved to the freezer for a longer storage time.

apple & ham biscuits

Makes 12 to 15 biscuits

Biscuits are easy to make, but are often overlooked as an everyday breakfast item. These biscuits are made in a very traditional way—with a generous portion of very cold butter cut into flour and baked—with slightly cooked diced apples added to the dough, resulting in a soft apple-y mouthful. Instead of buttermilk, however, these are made with plain yogurt. Yogurt works just as well and is a more common ingredient; most kitchens won't have buttermilk around on a daily basis.

The secret to amazing biscuits is handling the dough as little as possible. The dough may seem like it will fall apart easily, but that's what you're going for. The big bits of butter guarantee light and airy biscuits, perfect for stuffing with a slice of country ham.

SUGGESTED VARIETIES: *I like a softer apple here, so it blends with the biscuits. Try Sonata, Winesap, or Golden Delicious.*

BISCUITS

1 tablespoon unsalted butter

2 cups diced apple

4 cups all-purpose flour, plus more for counter

1 teaspoon sugar

1 teaspoon baking soda

1 tablespoon baking powder

1 teaspoon salt

1 cup (2 sticks) unsalted butter, chilled and cut into small cubes

1 cup cold plain yogurt

⅓ cup cold water

HAM

1 tablespoon unsalted butter

1½ pounds ham steak, cut into 12 equal pieces

Preheat the oven to 350 degrees F.

To prepare the biscuits: Add the butter to a medium sauté pan, and set over medium heat. Once the butter is melted completely, add the apple and cook until just soft, stirring often, about 5 minutes. Transfer the cooked apples to a plate in a single layer and move to the fridge to cool quickly and completely.

In the bowl of a food processor, add the flour, sugar, baking soda, baking powder, and salt. Pulse a few times to blend well. Open the top of the processor and scatter the butter cubes evenly over the surface of the flour mixture. Close and pulse about 30 times, until the dough resembles coarse crumbs. Open the top of the processor and scatter the

cooled apple over the surface.

In a small bowl, combine the yogurt and water, stirring until blended. While simultaneously pulsing the food processor, add the yogurt mixture through the tube until the dough is just starting to come together, about another 30 times. The dough will blend itself into 2 or 3 large portions.

Flour a countertop liberally, adding a spoonful to your hands to prevent sticking, and turn the dough out onto the counter. Using your palms, push together the large portions of dough, forming a single mass. Turn and form a rectangular block by pushing in the opposite sides of the dough. Do not knead.

Flour a rolling pin, and roll out the dough to about a ¾-inch thickness, working from the center. Using a 4-inch biscuit cutter or straight-edged drinking glass, cut as many biscuits as possible and place on a baking sheet, leaving at least 2 inches between biscuits. Any leftover dough can be pushed into a rectangle and recut into biscuits.

Bake until the biscuits are just starting to brown, about 20 minutes. Set aside to cool slightly.

To prepare the ham: While the biscuits are cooling, heat a large sauté pan over medium-high heat and add the butter. Once the butter is melted, place as many ham slices as you can fit into a single layer and sear on one side until golden brown. Remove from the pan and continue cooking in this fashion until all of the ham is browned.

To serve, split the biscuits in half and add a warm ham slice to each.

pumpkin seed muesli with apple-lime yogurt

Serves 6

Muesli is essentially pared-down granola. This dry grain cereal lacks the sweet crunch of other granolas (from binding with maple syrup or honey), making muesli a leaner and more nutritious version. I prefer my morning grain this way and like to serve muesli over a bowl of cool, plain yogurt. Tossing the apple slices with a squeeze of lime and a spoon of honey adds a sour-sweet-crisp element that will leave you craving more.

SUGGESTED VARIETIES: *Sweet, crispy apples are a nice complement to the tangy yogurt. Try Pink Lady, Fuji, or Honeycrisp.*

APPLE-LIME YOGURT

1 apple, cored

1 tablespoon honey, plus more for serving

Juice from ½ lime

2 sprigs fresh mint, finely chopped

6 cups plain yogurt

MUESLI

1 cup rolled oats

1 cup green pumpkin seeds

¼ cup sesame seeds

½ cup candied ginger, finely chopped

¼ teaspoon Chinese five-spice powder or ground cinnamon

Preheat the oven to 350 degrees F.

To prepare the Apple-Lime Yogurt: Slice the apple into thin half-moons and put them in a small bowl. Stir in the honey, lime juice, and chopped mint. Set aside.

To prepare the muesli: Spread the oats on a sheet pan. Place this in the oven and toast for 5 minutes. Add the pumpkin seeds and return the pan to the oven for another 5 minutes. The pumpkin seeds will pop as they toast. Add the sesame seeds and toast for 2 minutes more, until the oats, pumpkin seeds, and sesame seeds are fragrant. Remove the pan from the oven and toss, redistributing the muesli into a single layer. Let cool. Add the ginger and Chinese five-spice powder and stir to combine well.

Put 1 cup of yogurt in a shallow bowl for each serving. Add a handful of muesli and a few slices of apple fanned out on top. Drizzle with honey and serve.

Cooled leftover muesli can be stored in the pantry, in a sealed container, for about 3 weeks.

salads, starters & sides

apple bisteeya

Makes 18 to 24 medium-size turnovers

Bisteeya is a traditional Middle Eastern dish made with ground meat and a verdant spice mixture. The sweetness from apples naturally complements these homey spices. You can shape phyllo however you like for this recipe without affecting the flavor in any way. Stuffed triangle pockets are easy and allow for a generous amount of filling, but a rolled cigarette, cutout round, or small bite-sized triangle will work well, also.

SUGGESTED VARIETIES: *Cooking apples that break down easily and have a bit of tartness work well here. Try Gravenstein, Jonathan, or Empire.*

---

2 tablespoons olive oil

½ cup (1 stick) unsalted butter, divided

1 large red onion, finely chopped

2 medium apples, cored and cut into medium dice

1 tablespoon ground cinnamon

1 tablespoon ground coriander

1 tablespoon ground cumin

1 tablespoon fennel seeds, ground

½ teaspoon ground cloves

½ teaspoon red pepper flakes

1 teaspoon salt

¾ pound ground beef, no more than 85% lean

¼ cup raisins, chopped

½ cup toasted and ground almonds

8 sheets phyllo

¼ cup sesame seeds (optional)

In a large sauté pan, add the olive oil and 2 tablespoons of the butter, and set over medium-high heat. When the butter is melted, add the onion and cook with a pinch of salt until the onion is cooked through and beginning to brown and caramelize. You want a nice golden color, so don't rush—10 to 12 minutes total. Add the diced apples and all of the spices to the pan and cook, stirring occasionally, for about 5 minutes. Add the ground beef and cook until it is browned, the apples are soft and cooked through, and the pan is getting dry, 5 to 7 minutes. Remove from the heat and add the raisins and almonds. Set aside to cool.

Preheat the oven to 350 degrees F.

While the filling is cooling, prepare the phyllo. In a small pan, melt the remaining 6 tablespoons butter over low heat. You do not want to brown the butter at all. Set the phyllo sheets on the counter and cover with a damp cloth. Place 1 sheet at a time on your countertop and use a pastry brush to cover the entire sheet with butter. Place a second sheet of phyllo over the first, and repeat—brushing a thin layer of butter over the entire sheet.

Continue working in this way until you have 4 sheets stacked together. Cut sheet into even squares, about 5 inches long and 4 inches wide. You should have 9 to 12 phyllo squares. Discard any leftover trimmed phyllo. Spoon a generous amount of cooled filling into the center, leaving ½ inch around the edges. Fold the phyllo over, shape it into a triangle, and press the edges together to seal. Move the triangles to a baking sheet and set aside. To form more bisteeya, start again from the beginning, layering phyllo, cutting it down and filling it, until all filling is used.

When the pastries are ready, brush their tops with the last of the melted butter and sprinkle with sesame seeds, if using. Bake in the oven until golden brown and crispy, 40 to 45 minutes. Let cool slightly before serving.

apple fennel gratin

Serves 4

This recipe is quite humble, allowing the flavor of the apple and fennel to really shine through. Thinly sliced apples and fennel bulb are layered in a neat circle in a pie pan and covered with a bit of nutmeg-scented heavy cream—easy as that! The gratin bakes up into a thickened pot of velvety ingredients, a perfect side dish to any protein or a green salad as a delicate lunch.

SUGGESTED VARIETIES: *Apples that maintain their flavor with cooking are best for the gratin. Try Jonagold, Pink Lady, or Sonata.*

---

2 medium apples, cored

2 fennel bulbs, fronds trimmed and discarded

1 teaspoon salt

1 teaspoon freshly ground pepper

1 cup heavy cream

¼ teaspoon ground nutmeg

Preheat the oven to 350 degrees F.

Using a mandoline or sharp knife, shave thin sections of apple, about ⅛ inch thick. Put the apple slices in a large bowl. Repeat with the fennel bulb, slicing crosswise into slightly thicker pieces, and add to the bowl. Add the salt and pepper and toss with your hands to evenly season all slices.

In a shallow pie pan or baking dish, layer apples on the bottom in a circle, overlapping the edges slightly. Repeat with a layer of fennel bulb. Continue working in this fashion until all of the apple and fennel have been added. Pour the heavy cream over the top of the slices and press them down strongly to compress. Sprinkle the nutmeg evenly over the top of the gratin and bake until golden brown and soft, 45 to 60 minutes. Serve immediately.

EAST VERSUS WEST: A REGIONAL APPLE GUIDE

Apple trees, like any plant, have preferred habitats and are prolific only when the environment suits the breed. Because of this phenomenon, apple varieties vary across planting zones, and therefore across the United States. Apples that are common in New England may not do well in the Pacific Northwest and vice versa. Washington and New York are the first and second largest producers of apples nationally, and local apple varieties in each region will vary. Following is a list of regional apple varieties.

SOUTHEAST: Virginia Beauty, York, Albemarle Pippin, Spitzenburg, Yates, Mountain Boomer.

GREATER GREAT LAKES AND INTERIOR NORTHEAST: Pristine, Dayton, Akane, Shay, Enterprise, Liberty, Melrose, Gravenstein, William's Pride, Belmac, Wolf River.

NORTHEAST: Northern Spy, Baldwin, Smokehouse, King David, Arkansas, Newtown Pippin.

NORTHERN MIDWEST: Apple varieties that do well in the cooler zones of the North are typically hardy varieties. Look for Zestar, SnowSweet, Red Flesh, Honeycrisp, Wolf River, Dolgo, Centennial, Arkansas Black, Liberty, Spitzenburg, Gravenstein.

SOUTHERN MIDWEST: The milder climate of the southern states assures that a larger variety of apples do well. Many apples will prosper in this region; popular varieties are Gravenstein, Jonagold, Liberty, Akane, Queen Cox.

PACIFIC NORTHWEST: Warmer winters and cooler summers offer excellent growing conditions for apples. Heirloom varieties to seek out include Akane, Liberty, Shay, Pristine, Chehalis, Williams' Pride, Dayton, Fiesta, Queen Cox, Resi, Rajka.

sautéed brussels sprouts & apples

Serves 2 to 4

This recipe is super simple to make and highlights the flavors of each ingredient. Pairing bitter Brussels sprouts with sweet fall apples creates a nice contrast. The secret to this dish is allowing the Brussels sprouts to brown, coaxing out their sweetness. Apple bits are tossed in during the last few minutes of cooking—just enough time to cook the fruit through without it breaking down. All in all, you are aiming for a perfectly al dente dish here, where natural flavors reign. The addition of toasted pine nuts warms it up and adds heartiness.

SUGGESTED VARIETIES: *Select firm apples that retain their shape when cooked. Try Pippin, Cortland, or Granny Smith.*

¼ cup pine nuts

2 tablespoons olive oil

1 tablespoon unsalted butter

½ pound Brussels sprouts, halved (about 2 cups)

1 medium apple, cut into equal-sized large dice (about 1 cup)

Salt and freshly ground pepper

In a small sauté pan, toast the pine nuts over medium heat until brown, about 3 minutes.

In a medium saucepan, add the olive oil and butter over medium-high heat. When the butter is fully melted and starting to foam, add the Brussels sprouts in a single layer. (It's okay if they overlap slightly, but do not let them get more than 2 layers deep.) Turn the heat down to medium and cook, leaving the sprouts undisturbed, for 4 minutes. Don't stir! This allows the bottoms to brown and caramelize. After 4 minutes, stir the sprouts completely, so the browned sides are mostly up. Leave in the pan to caramelize undisturbed for another 4 minutes.

When the sprouts are browned on both sides, stir again and add the diced apples. Stir every 2 minutes or so until the apples are just soft, about 6 minutes more. Add the toasted pine nuts, season to taste with salt and pepper, and serve.

apple fry bread with carrot hummus

Serves 6 as an appetizer

Made in the fashion of a traditional Indian bread, this fry bread is stuffed with a thick layer of apple paste, savory green onions, and sesame oil before being fried up into a bubbly and doughy crisp. A cumin-scented savory carrot "hummus" is served on the side, making this a flavorful and robust appetizer or a filling lunch. Yogurt gives the dough a nice, rich body, but be sure to roll it thin. You're going more for a slim layer of dough than a calzone-like pocket.

SUGGESTED VARIETIES: *Try McIntosh, Spitzenburg, Rome, and Empire or any combination of these for a deeply apple-flavored paste.*

---

2 medium apples, cored and cut into 1-inch pieces

½ cup water

CARROT HUMMUS

4 carrots, peeled and cut into 1-inch pieces

3 cloves garlic, peeled and smashed

4 tablespoons olive oil, divided

1 teaspoon ground cumin

Salt and freshly ground pepper

FRY BREAD

2 cups all-purpose flour, plus more for rolling

½ teaspoon baking soda

½ teaspoon salt

1 cup plain yogurt

4 green onions, whites and greens chopped to measure 5 tablespoons

1 teaspoon toasted sesame oil

¼ cup vegetable oil, plus more as needed

Preheat the oven to 350 degrees F.

In a large pot, add the apples and water. Bring to a boil then reduce the heat to a simmer and cover the pot, cooking until the apples are very soft and easily smashed with a fork, about 20 minutes. Add the apples and liquid to a blender and puree until smooth, about 1 minute. Return the apple puree to the pot and cook over low heat until thick and paste-like. When the apple paste is sticking to the bottom of the pan slightly, and very thick, scoop it into a small bowl and put in the fridge to cool completely.

To prepare the Carrot Hummus: While the apples are cooling, toss the carrot pieces and garlic with 3 tablespoons of the olive oil and spread out on a sheet pan. Roast until soft, about 25 minutes. Put in a blender or food processor with the remaining tablespoon of olive oil and the cumin. Process until smooth. Season with salt and pepper to taste, and set aside in a small serving bowl.

To prepare the fry bread: While the carrots are roasting, make the dough. Put the flour, baking soda, salt, and yogurt in the bowl of an electric mixer fitted with the paddle attachment. Mix until well combined and the dough is smooth, pulling away from the sides of the bowl, about 5 minutes. Remove the dough from the bowl and knead on a lightly floured countertop until smooth and elastic. Set aside, covered with a dish towel or piece of plastic wrap, until you're ready to use it, at least 30 minutes. In a small bowl, stir together the green onions and sesame oil and set aside.

Divide the dough into 6 even pieces, about 3 ounces each. Lightly flour the countertop and roll out each piece of dough thinly, about 8 inches in diameter. Spoon about a table-spoon of apple paste over the surface of the dough and sprinkle with some of the green onion mixture. Fold the dough in half, forming a half-moon. Working from the center, press out the air and press the edges together to seal.

Heat the vegetable oil in a large sauté pan over medium heat. When the oil is hot, add the shaped fry bread and cook the first side until it's puffed up and brown, about 3 minutes. Using tongs or a spatula, flip over to brown the second side, about 3 minutes more. Remove the bread from the pan and transfer to a baking sheet. Set aside.

Continue forming and frying the dough in this fashion until all 6 pieces are browned and on the sheet pan. Put the sheet pan in the oven and bake until cooked through completely about, 10 minutes. Let the bread cool about 5 minutes before cutting. Slice each piece of bread into 4 equal triangles and serve alongside the Carrot Hummus.

apple & red lentil steamed dumplings

Makes about 3 dozen

These are nontraditional dumplings, to be sure! Smashed red lentils are combined with toasted Indian spices for a strongly scented filling, then combined with fresh apples for a bright flavor. The intensely flavored lentil filling is added to the center of an Asian dumpling wrapper and steamed. These small packets of savory ingredients are perfect for appetizers or make a tasty and healthy lunch. You can also form and freeze the dumplings, uncooked, for another time.

SUGGESTED VARIETIES: *Crisp and sweet apples work well in these dumplings, so the flavor really shines through. Try Honeycrisp, Gala, or Sonata.*

---

2 cups homemade stock or water

1 cup red lentils

¼ cup coconut or vegetable oil

½ teaspoon fenugreek seeds

½ teaspoon black mustard seeds

½ teaspoon fennel seeds

½ teaspoon red pepper flakes

½ teaspoon coriander seeds

½ teaspoon cumin seeds

1-inch-long piece of fresh gingerroot, peeled and finely diced (about 1 tablespoon)

1 clove garlic, roughly chopped

½ teaspoon salt

¼ teaspoon ground cinnamon

½ large yellow onion, finely diced

3 medium apples, cored and finely diced

1 package wonton wrappers

In a medium saucepan, add the stock and lentils and bring to a boil; cover the pan, reduce the heat to low and simmer. Be sure to check that the lentils are not sticking, and add small amounts of stock or water as needed. Cook until the lentils are perfectly soft, 25 to 30 minutes. They will fall apart and come together in a soft mash.

Meanwhile, in a small sauté pan, heat the coconut oil over medium-high heat until it's hot. Stir in the fenugreek, black mustard, fennel, red pepper, coriander, and cumin. When the spices begin to pop, about 4 minutes, add the ginger, garlic, salt, cinnamon, and onion, cooking and stirring until soft and slightly caramelized, 6 to 8 minutes. Set aside.

Once the lentils are soft, remove the pot from the heat and add the diced apples. Replace the cover and let sit to soften the apples, about 10 minutes. Once the apples have softened slightly, add the spice-oil mixture and stir well to combine. Leave the pot uncovered on the countertop or in the fridge until the lentils are completely cool.

Once the lentils are cool and thick, prepare to form your dumplings. Set a small bowl of water on the countertop and lay out 6 to 8 wonton wrappers, leaving space between. Using a small spoon, place about a teaspoon of lentils in the center of a wrapper. Moisten all 4 edges of the wrapper and with both hands, form the dumplings into a pouch by pinching the dumpling between your thumbs and forefingers. (You can make any dumpling shape you prefer.) Set the formed dumpling aside and continue making the dumplings in this fashion until all the filling is used. Do not moisten more than 2 wrappers at a time, lest they dry and weaken before you can form them.

Set a steamer basket in a pot over high heat and bring water to a boil. Brush the bottom of the steamer basket with a light coat of oil so the wrappers will not stick. Place as many dumplings as you can fit into the basket, being sure to leave a little space between them, and steam until the wrappers are translucent and cooked through, about 10 minutes for each batch. Continue cooking the dumplings in this fashion until they are all done, serving as they are finished and still hot from the steamer.

apple-fig bread pudding

Serves 6

This savory bread pudding is a bit like a traditional holiday stuffing, but gets sweetened up with the addition of apples and figs. Sharp cheddar cheese is added for heartiness and a bit of bite. This is a stick-to-your-ribs dish that can be eaten at room temperature for an easy lunch or enjoyed straight from the oven.

SUGGESTED VARIETIES: *I like a softer apple that will break down a bit. Try Sonata, Winesap, or Golden Delicious.*

---

8 ounces bread, cut into 1-inch cubes, (about 2 cups)

1 cup milk

2 tablespoons olive oil

1 tablespoon unsalted butter

1 large onion, chopped into 1-inch pieces

1 shallot, chopped

1 teaspoon salt

½ teaspoon freshly ground pepper

2 sprigs fresh sage (about 10 leaves)

2 medium apples, cored and diced

10 dried figs, finely chopped

2 tablespoons vermouth, sherry, or white wine

2 large eggs, beaten

1 cup (about 4 ounces) grated sharp cheddar

In a large bowl, add the bread cubes and milk. Set aside to let the bread absorb the liquid.

Set a large sauté pan over medium-high heat and add the oil and butter. When the butter is melted, add the onion, shallot, salt, and pepper. Cook until the onion is softened and just beginning to brown, 6 to 8 minutes. Add the sage and stir to combine. Add the apples and figs and continue sautéing until the apples are softening and just cooked through, about 10 minutes. Add the vermouth to deglaze the pan, scraping up any brown bits. Once the vermouth has evaporated, about 1 minute, set the pan aside to cool.

Preheat the oven to 350 degrees F.

Once the apple mixture is cool, add it to the bowl of soaked bread and stir to combine. Pour over the beaten eggs and cheese and stir, distributing the ingredients evenly.

Put the bread pudding in an 8 x 8-inch baking dish, pressing down to fit it all in. Bake for 40 minutes, until golden brown. If the bread cubes brown too quickly, cover the pudding loosely with foil. Serve immediately.

apple & winter squash tian

Serves 4

A tian is a shallow earthenware baking dish, but any shallow baking dish will work in this recipe. Tians are very similar to gratins, but tend to have exposed fruits or vegetables whose edges, left uncovered, crisp up and caramelize. The beauty of a tian is in the presentation, so take care to cut your apples and squash precisely and layer them in neat rows.

SUGGESTED VARIETIES: *Select firm apples that retain their shape when cooked. Try Pippin, Cortland, or Granny Smith.*

---

1 medium butternut squash neck (about 10 to 12 ounces), peeled

3 medium apples, cored

1 cup heavy cream

1 teaspoon salt

1 teaspoon freshly ground pepper

¼ cup (about 1 ounce) grated Parmesan

¼ cup chopped fresh parsley

¼ cup chopped fresh thyme

1 tablespoon olive oil

Preheat the oven to 375 degrees F.

Prepare the butternut squash by slicing the neck in half lengthwise. Slice into thin half-moons. Prepare the apples by slicing each in half lengthwise. Slice into thin half-moons.

In a medium bowl, combine the cream, salt, pepper, Parmesan, parsley, and thyme. Set aside.

Butter a glass pie pan or baking dish. Stack the apple and squash slices vertically in the pan with the flat edges of the slices along the bottom of the pan. Alternate squash and apples and work in tidy rows, resulting in a pretty, evenly domed tian. Pour the heavy cream mixture between the rows. The cream should come almost to the top of the pan, but will not cover the slices completely. Brush the tops of the apples and squash with olive oil.

Bake until the squash and apples are completely cooked through and golden brown, 35 to 40 minutes. Serve immediately.

EAT FRESH

Not all apples are created equal. Some are better for baking, others are best for storing, while some work only as juice. Have you ever eaten a crab apple fresh off the tree? Not good. Just as there are apples best for juicing or baking, it's equally true that particular apples are best eaten fresh. Spare them from pies or sauces; some crispy sweet apples are made for biting into immediately.

Fresh eating apples should maintain a generous level of juiciness. (This juiciness may not hold when cooking.) They are also well-balanced apples with a strong apple flavor that will be lost after cooking.

The most common eating apple (that is often frowned upon for baking) is the Red Delicious. Brilliant, deep red apple skin gives way to a crisp, moderately sweet eating apple. These juicy fruits do not maintain their flavor if cooked, and tend to go grainy, but they are a perfect eating apple and are available nationwide.

Other common eat-fresh standouts include the big, crispy, and sweet Fuji, the Gala (which is thick-skinned), and the perfect sweet-crisp blends Cameo and Honeycrisp.

cumin apple salad with pickled red onions

Serves 4 to 6

This refreshing salad is perfect for fall and winter months when lettuce greens are in short supply. Sweet apples, cut into matchsticks, are paired with crispy romaine and vinegar-spiked red onions that combine into a perfect forkful with every bite. Pickling the onions in advance mellows their flavor and keeps them from overpowering the salad. Leaving the apples in long slivers ensures that their flavor will shine through and hold up to the vinegar.

SUGGESTED VARIETIES: *Fresh-eating apples are best in salads. Try Cameo, Honeycrisp, or Crimson Delight.*

½ small red onion, thinly sliced	1 medium apple, julienned
½ cup red wine vinegar	¼ teaspoon ground cumin
1 bunch radishes, cleaned and trimmed	⅛ teaspoon salt
½ head romaine lettuce	⅛ teaspoon freshly ground pepper
1 orange, segmented	3 tablespoons olive oil

Put the onion slices in a small bowl and pour the red wine vinegar over them. Set aside for 15 minutes.

Using the largest side of a box grater, grate the radishes, measuring out 1 cup. Put the grated radishes in a large bowl. Separate the romaine leaves and cut in half along the wide center rib. Then cut the leaves into 2-inch-wide strips. Add the lettuce to the bowl with the radishes. Add the orange segments and apple.

Drain the vinegar from the onion, reserving 2 tablespoons, and add the onion and reserved vinegar to the salad. Add the cumin, salt, pepper, and olive oil and toss well to coat the greens. Serve immediately.

grated green apple salad

Serves 4 to 6

This salad is flavorful and gorgeous in its simplicity. Sour green apples are grated, and seasoned with a touch of sugar, and scented with orange blossom water. The floral notes complement simply roasted fish dishes or work as a refreshing after-meal palate cleanser. You can find orange blossom water in the ethnic section of most grocery stores and in most specialty cooking shops.

SUGGESTED VARIETIES: *Choose a tart green apple for this salad. Try Granny Smith or Gravenstein.*

---

2 large green apples, cored and grated

1 tablespoon fresh lemon juice

3 tablespoons sugar

¼ cup finely chopped fresh mint

1 teaspoon orange blossom water

In a large bowl, add the grated apples and lemon juice. Toss to combine and let sit for 10 minutes. After the apples have macerated, add the sugar, chopped mint, and orange blossom water; fold to combine well. Stir until all of the sugar has dissolved. Chill, covered, until you're ready to serve, at least 30 minutes. In summer, you can also serve immediately and add a few ice cubes to the bowl to chill it, where they will melt and add to the apple "broth."

SIMPLE APPLESAUCE

Applesauce is a kid crowd pleaser. The slightly sweet taste and smashed texture work well with their palates, making applesauce is a safe bet for snacking. Fortunately, applesauce is super easy to make at home, and it's a great project for letting kids loose in the kitchen without much worry. The simplicity of cooking apples slowly in water keeps kids safe and parents relaxed.

Apples that are misshapen or slightly bruised are perfect for this recipe. If you're shopping at the farmers' market, look around for "seconds"—fruits that command a lower price due to their appearance.

Kids can take charge at various steps along the way. If you have older children, set them to work slicing by way of an apple slicer. These round cutters have large plastic handles, which are easy to hang on to while pushing down on the apple to cut. No knife skills needed! Smaller children can assemble other ingredients and help to stir the apples once they're cooking. However, the best chore for kids is the smashing. Applesauce is can be made several different ways: pureed in a blender (which produces a smooth paste), mashed with a potato masher by hand (resulting in a chunkier texture), or pushing through a food mill (producing a balance of slightly chunky and slightly smooth sauce).

Makes 4 cups

4 pounds apples, peeled, cored, and
  chopped into small pieces

1 lemon, juiced

1 teaspoon ground cinnamon

1 cup water

½ cup sugar (optional)

Put the apples, lemon juice, cinnamon, and water in a large pot and set over medium-high heat. Bring the apples to a boil and then reduce the heat to a simmer. Stir the apples often, and smash them with a wooden spoon as they begin to break down. Cook until all of the apples are completely soft and falling apart, 30 to 45 minutes. Taste to see if sugar is needed. If so, add in small increments until the flavor is balanced. Remove the apples from the heat and let them cool completely before handling.

To smooth the apples into sauce, have kids scoop apple mash into a blender or food mill. Process until the desired consistency is reached. Store in the fridge until you're ready to use, up to 3 weeks.

apple & celery salad with toasted hazelnuts

Serves 4

This salad is perfect for fall and winter eating, as both apples and celery are fresh and crisp. It's a nice light counterpoint to all the roasted meats and hearty sautéed greens of the season. This is also the perfect salad for a crowd, because you can prepare the apples sticks and celery in advance, covering them with a damp cloth and holding them in the fridge. The vinaigrette can be made ahead, as well, and you can toss everything together just before serving. Dill punctuates the sweetness of the apples, and toasted hazelnuts add a lush fatty note to this otherwise lean dish.

SUGGESTED VARIETIES: *Choose a good fresh-eating apple for this salad: Pink Lady, Cameo, or Honeycrisp.*

---

1 shallot, finely diced	¼ cup olive oil
1 tablespoon apple cider vinegar	½ teaspoon Dijon mustard
½ teaspoon salt	½ teaspoon honey
¼ teaspoon freshly ground pepper	2 tablespoons finely chopped fresh dill
2 celery stalks plus leaves	½ cup chopped hazelnuts, toasted
1 large apple	

Put the shallot in a medium bowl and add the apple cider vinegar, salt, and pepper. Set aside. (Allowing the shallot to sit for a short time in vinegar pickles it slightly while also mellowing the flavor, removing the oniony bite.)

Cut the celery into very thin slices, using a mandoline if you have one. Set the apple on a cutting board and cut as close to the core as possible, slicing a large segment off the side. Rotate and cut off another side, as close to the core as possible. Continue cutting in this fashion until you have 4 big pieces and a square-shaped core. Dispose of the core and place the flat side of each apple piece against the cutting board. Cut into thin slices. Then turn that stack of sliced apple on its side and cut into matchsticks.

Add the olive oil, mustard, and honey to the bowl with the shallots and stir to combine. When everything is well incorporated, add the celery, apple, and dill. Fold all of the ingredients together, coating evenly with the vinaigrette. Sprinkle the hazelnuts over the top and serve immediately.

mains

butternut squash & apple soup

Serves 4

Butternut squash is a winter staple and purees to a velvety soup in a short amount of time. The addition of apples lightens the bowl and produces a sweet scent to complement the squash. Warming spices are added for a savory note, making this soup perfect for a quick dinner or easy lunch. Garnish with a dollop of plain yogurt and toasted squash seeds for a pretty finish to a fall-inspired meal.

SUGGESTED VARIETIES: *Cooking apples that break down easily and have a bit of tartness work well here. Try Gravenstein, Jonathan, or Empire.*

---

2 tablespoons olive oil

1 medium onion, diced

1 teaspoon salt

1 small butternut squash (about 2 pounds), peeled, seeded, and cut into 1-inch chunks

4 cups chicken or vegetable stock or water

2 medium apples, cored and cut into small pieces

1 teaspoon ground cumin

1 teaspoon ground fennel

1 teaspoon ground coriander

Salt and freshly ground pepper

Plain yogurt, for serving

Toasted pumpkin seeds, for serving

In a large stockpot, warm the olive oil over medium heat. Add the onion and salt, stirring until the onion is soft but not brown, about 2 minutes. Add the squash and stir occasionally, letting the pieces sit still and brown a bit (the onion will start caramelizing, as well), 8 to 10 minutes. Pour in the stock and add the apple pieces and spices. Reduce the heat to low and simmer until the squash and apples are soft and cooked through, about 30 minutes. Remove from the heat.

Carefully add the soup to a blender, in batches. Remember to leave room in the blender—liquids expand when heated. Puree until smooth, adding a bit of water if you'd like a thinner consistency. Season with salt and pepper to taste. Garnish with a spoonful of yogurt and pumpkin seeds, if desired, and serve immediately.

chicken curry salad with apples & parsley

Serves 2 to 4

This chicken salad is wildly simple to make but packs in amazing fresh flavor. The combination of apples and large tears of parsley leaves make this dish feel light and healthy. With just enough mayonnaise to bind all of the ingredients, this flavorful salad is a virtuous lunch and stores well in the fridge for a few days. Raisins increase the sweet factor, but can be omitted, while a hearty portion of curry powder infuses the dish with a subtle perfume and shouldn't be scrimped on. This is also an excellent recipe for using any leftover roasted chicken.

SUGGESTED VARIETIES: *Fresh-eating apples that are sweet work well with curry. Try Gala, Cortland, or Honeycrisp.*

---

2 cups chicken stock

½ pound boneless skinless chicken breast

½ cup mayonnaise

1 teaspoon curry powder

¼ teaspoon paprika

¼ teaspoon salt

¼ teaspoon freshly ground pepper

1 medium apple, cored and cut into small dice

1 tablespoon raisins, chopped

½ cup torn fresh parsley leaves

In a small saucepan, add the chicken stock and set over medium-high heat. When the stock is just starting to bubble, reduce the heat to medium and submerge the chicken breast in the broth. Cook, turning once, for about 15 minutes, until the chicken is totally cooked through and firm. Remove the chicken breast from the stock and set on a plate to cool. (Strain and save any leftover stock for another use.)

Once it's cool, cut the poached chicken into 1-inch dice and add to a medium bowl. Add the mayonnaise, curry, paprika, salt, and pepper; fold together until the ingredients are well mixed and the spices are evenly incorporated. Add the apple, raisins, and parsley leaves; fold together until just combined. Serve the salad stuffed in a pita, on sandwich bread, or plated with a green salad on the side.

spiced chickpea salad with apples & mint

Serves 6

A blend of crisp apples and herbs creates this flavorful and healthy legume salad. The vinaigrette is a dressing of olive oil, red wine vinegar, Dijon mustard, and plenty of herbs and spices. I prefer to use dried chickpeas (also known as garbanzo beans) that are cooked in this recipe, as they retain their shape and have a nice bite to them—canned beans can be too soft. The herbs and spices in this salad are the real star, and the apples lend a crisp texture. Cut the apples into a small and even dice, about the size of the chickpeas, which assures the perfect bite every time.

SUGGESTED VARIETIES: *Crisp and firm apples are best here, as they won't break down in the vinaigrette. Try Northern Spy, Honeycrisp, or Gala.*

---

2 cups dried chickpeas, soaked overnight

VINAIGRETTE
1 clove garlic, minced

¼ cup red wine vinegar

¼ cup olive oil

1 tablespoon Dijon mustard

1 teaspoon paprika

1 tablespoon chopped fresh or dried oregano

1 tablespoon chopped fresh or dried marjoram

1 tablespoon salt

1 tablespoon chopped fresh or dried mint

½ teaspoon salt

¼ teaspoon red pepper flakes

½ bunch Italian parsley, stemmed and chopped

2 medium apples, cored and cut into small dice

Drain the soaked chickpeas and put them in a large saucepan. Cover with water, add the salt, and bring to a boil. Reduce to a simmer and cook until the chickpeas are tender, 40 to 60 minutes. Drain and cool.

To prepare the vinaigrette: In a medium bowl, add the garlic and red wine vinegar and set aside for 5 minutes. Whisk in the olive oil, Dijon mustard, paprika, oregano, marjoram, mint, salt, and red pepper flakes.

Put the cooled chickpeas in a large serving bowl and cover with the dressing. Stir to combine. Fold in the parsley and apples. Let the salad stand for 30 minutes before serving, which will allow the flavors to develop.

apple & bacon strata

Serves 6

A strata is similar to a crustless quiche, but includes big cubes of rustic bread for a heartier version. This is a great use for leftover baguette or any bread you have that is past its prime. The cubes of bread soak up the egg mixture and bake into a soft egg-bread similar to French toast. Stratas are lovely when served for brunch, but also make a great weekday lunch alongside a green salad.

SUGGESTED VARIETIES: *Apples that maintain their flavor after cooking are best with the bacon. Try Jonagold, Pink Lady, or Crimson Delight.*

---

8 large eggs, beaten

½ cup milk

3 tablespoons fresh thyme leaves, chopped

½ teaspoon salt

¼ teaspoon freshly ground pepper

8 ounces rustic bread, cut into 2-inch cubes (about 2½ cups)

½ pound bacon, cut into ½-inch ribbons

1 tablespoon unsalted butter

½ medium yellow onion, finely chopped (about 1½ cups)

2 medium apples, cored and diced

Preheat the oven to 350 degrees F.

In a large mixing bowl, add the eggs, milk, thyme, salt, and pepper. Beat to incorporate the seasonings. Put half of the bread cubes into the eggs and soak.

Brown the bacon in a large sauté pan; once it's browned, transfer bacon to a paper towel and pour off all but 1 tablespoon of bacon fat from the pan. Add the butter and onion to the pan, and set over medium heat. Sauté until the onion is cooked through, 10 to 15 minutes. (This takes longer than usual because of the lower heat.) Once the onion is starting to brown, add the apples and stir until just cooked, about 10 minutes. Add the remaining bread cubes to the pan, remove from the heat, and stir gently until the onion mixture cools down.

Once the onion-apple mixture is cool, add it to the egg mixture and fold until all of the bread cubes are well coated in egg. Egg should pool in the bottom of the bowl. Put the mixture into a buttered shallow baking pan (a 9-inch rectangle or circle works well) and press down the bread cubes until they're fully submerged in the egg. Put in the oven and bake until the egg is completely cooked through and the top of the strata turns golden brown, about 45 minutes. Cool slightly before serving.

GROWING APPLES IN A CONTAINER

Traditionally, apple trees are planted in an orchard, with rows of knobby trees and low-hanging bows densely packed. Even in backyards, apple trees are grouped together (often alongside other fruit trees) as they need a cross pollinator in order to produce fruit. Over the past several years, however, growers have cultivated a new kind of apple tree that can be grown in a container.

Container apple trees are grafted onto dwarf rootstock. The term *stock* refers to the actual trunk and root of the tree. Choosing a dwarf rootstock keeps both the root structure and the branches—a near-miniature version of an apple tree. For anyone without much space, these dwarf trees may be the perfect solution for homegrown fruit. They do well on patios, balconies, and rooftops.

Many varieties of apple trees are available, but you must choose an appropriate tree for your growing region. Apple trees prefer a long, hard freeze overwinter, so if you live in a more mild climate you should choose a suitable stock. Apple trees can be planted as you would any other potted plant. Your potting soil should include compost or bark. These add a richness and texture to the soil and will help retain moisture.

Your local nursery should offer advice on how best to care for your potted apple tree, but it is worth noting that you will not see fruit in the first year. In the first season, removing any immature fruits that form ensures that a healthy root system will develop.

In addition to dwarf trees, columnar apple trees are now available for purchase. These trees are one tall column of tree trunk, with several very short branches jutting directly from the trunk. During the growing season, these spurs are covered in bunched leaves and fruit, making this tree a beauty to look at. Columnar trees are relatively productive, and their diminutive size makes them an excellent choice for small spaces.

savory barley-stuffed apples with rosemary

Makes 10 to 12 stuffed apples

Using apples at the center of a savory meal is another way to celebrate the season and liven up the dinner table. In this recipe, apples are cored and some flesh removed to create a pocket for stuffing. Roasted barley spiked with savory nuts and scented with fresh herbs acts as a substantial filler, making this a perfect vegetarian main dish, especially for the holiday table. Of course, you can also add some crumbled sausage or browned bacon to the mix, if you're so inclined. This is one recipe that is easily adaptable to other grains and flavors, so feel free to experiment.

SUGGESTED VARIETIES: *Any apple that bakes well but doesn't remain too crisp is perfect here. Try Sonata, Jonathan, or Honeycrisp.*

---

1 cup barley

3 cups water

2 tablespoons unsalted butter, divided

2 tablespoons olive oil

2 leeks, white and light green parts only, diced

½ teaspoon salt

½ teaspoon freshly ground pepper

1 carrot, peeled, and finely diced.

8 button mushrooms, finely diced

2 sprigs fresh rosemary, chopped (about 2 tablespoons)

10 sprigs fresh thyme, chopped (about 1 tablespoon)

½ cup walnuts, crushed

1 orange, zested and juiced

10 to 12 medium apples

In a medium saucepan, add the barley, water, and 1 tablespoon of the butter. Bring the mixture to a boil, then reduce it to a simmer and cook until the barley is just cooked through, 45 minutes to 1 hour.

Meanwhile, in a large sauté pan, add the olive oil and the remaining tablespoon of butter. When the butter is completely melted, add the leeks, salt, and pepper. Sauté until the leeks are soft and starting to brown slightly, 6 to 8 minutes. Add the carrot and sauté until al dente, about 3 minutes. Add the mushrooms and cook until they release their liquid and all of the ingredients start to brown, 8 to 10 minutes. The pan will be quite dry. Remove from the heat and stir in the chopped herbs, walnuts, and orange juice and zest. Set aside.

When the barley is finished cooking, drain the water well and stir the barley into the vegetable mixture. Taste for seasoning and add salt and pepper, if desired.

Preheat the oven to 350 degrees F. Grease a shallow roasting pan.

Using a small spoon or apple corer, core each apple, then scoop out its flesh to create a wide channel, but without cracking the top. The opening will be about 1-inch wide and run all the way down to the bottom of the apple. Fill each apple with several spoonfuls of stuffing, pressing down to pack in as much as possible. Add the filled apples to the roasting pan. Bake for 40 to 45 minutes, until the apples are cooked through and a knife will pierce their flesh easily. Cool slightly before serving.

fish tacos with cabbage & apple

Serves 6

Crispy and earthy cabbage is shredded super thin (with either a sharp knife or a mandoline) and paired with sweet apples in a subtly spicy vinaigrette. Make sure your cabbage is light and thin so you have a delicate mouthful instead of a thick crunch that will overwhelm the flavors.

SUGGESTED VARIETIES: *Choose a good fresh-eating apple for this salad: Pink Lady, Cameo, or Honeycrisp.*

---

12 corn tortillas

½ pound green cabbage, cored and shredded

3 to 4 medium apples, cored and thinly julienned

6 tablespoons olive oil, divided

2 tablespoons apple cider vinegar

1 teaspoon Dijon mustard

1 tablespoon honey

¼ teaspoon cayenne pepper

2 teaspoons salt

1½ pounds halibut, cut into 4 fillets

½ teaspoon freshly ground pepper

FOR GARNISH (OPTIONAL):

Chopped fresh cilantro

Diced jalapeño

Lime slices

Preheat the oven to 250 degrees F. Lightly moisten a dish towel and wrap the tortillas in it. Put in the warmed oven and hold until you're ready to serve.

In a large mixing bowl, add the shredded cabbage, apples, 4 tablespoons of the olive oil, the apple cider vinegar, Dijon, honey, cayenne, and 1 teaspoon of the salt. Toss the ingredients, using both hands or a large spoon. Stir very well until the ingredients are well combined and the cabbage is evenly coated. Set aside for at least 30 minutes.

While the cabbage is macerating, prepare the fish. Season the halibut fillets with the remaining teaspoon of salt and the pepper. In a large sauté pan, heat the remaining 2 tablespoons of olive oil over medium-high heat. When the oil is hot and rippling, add the fish fillets, being sure not to overcrowd the pan. Cook, without moving, for 4 minutes, until crispy and deep golden brown. Turn the fish and cook the other side until crisp and brown, about another 4 minutes. The fish is done when it is flaky and opaque.

Remove the fish from the pan chop into cubes, and place it on a platter to serve. Serve the fish alongside cabbage, a plate of warmed tortillas, and any garnishes you're using; let everyone build their own tacos.

prosciutto-and-apple-wrapped fish with potato crisps

Serves 4

This dish is elegant, but it is also super easy to make. Prosciutto is layered with overlapping paper-thin apple slices to create a flavorful envelope around a fish fillet. From start to finish, this recipe will come together in less than 30 minutes. If you have fresh herbs available, layer them between the fish and the apples to really up the flavor—sage works particularly well.

SUGGESTED VARIETIES: *Apples that maintain their flavor after cooking are best with the prosciutto. Try Jonagold, Pink Lady, or Sonata.*

---

4 slices prosciutto

1 medium apple, cored and cut paper-thin with a mandoline or sharp knife

Four 5-ounce portions of firm white fish, such as halibut or monkfish

½ teaspoon freshly ground pepper

4 tablespoons olive oil, divided

1 tablespoon unsalted butter

1 pound small white potatoes such as Yukon gold or fingerling sliced in half lengthwise

Salt

Preheat the oven to 350 degrees F.

On a countertop, lay flat each piece of prosciutto. Layer the apple slices over the prosciutto, overlapping the edges and covering the entire piece. Season the fish with pepper and place each, skin-side up, in the middle of a prosciutto slice. Fold up the edges of the prosciutto and apples, covering the fish entirely. Set aside.

In a large ovenproof sauté pan over medium heat, heat 2 tablespoons of the olive oil with the butter. When the butter is melted and hot, add the potatoes to the pan in a single layer, cut-side down. Sprinkle with some salt and cook until the bottoms are golden brown, about 8 minutes. The potatoes will still give resistance and be raw in the middle. Put the entire pan in the oven and bake until completely cooked through, another 15 minutes.

While the potatoes are cooking, put the remaining 2 tablespoons olive oil in another large ovenproof sauté pan and set over medium heat. When oil is hot, add the wrapped fish, seam-side down. Cook until the prosciutto is just brown, about 4 minutes. Turn the fish over and brown the other side, about 4 minutes. Put the pan of fish in the oven next to the potatoes and continue cooking until the fish is firm and cooked through, another 8 to 10 minutes.

Transfer the fish and potatoes to a serving platter. Serve immediately.

root vegetable & apple pie with sausage

Serves 4 to 6

This hearty apple and vegetable pie smacks of winter and is delicious for brunch, lunch, or dinner. I like to use golden beets in this recipe, as red beets give the appearance of a sweet pie after baking, but feel free to use any beet you prefer. Phyllo is used as a crispy crust here, layered with root vegetables and apples in a savory pie.

SUGGESTED VARIETIES: *Many apples will work well in this recipe—both those that hold their shape and those that break down. I like Pippin, Rome, or Granny Smith.*

---

1 tablespoon olive oil

1 large yellow onion

½ pound ground Italian sausage, casings removed

½ cup (1 stick) unsalted butter

10 sheets phyllo

2 to 3 golden beets (about ½ pound), peeled and thinly sliced, about ⅛ inch thick

¼ teaspoon salt

¼ teaspoon freshly ground pepper

3 to 4 medium apples (about 1 pound), cored and thinly sliced, about ¼ inch thick

2 to 3 turnips (about ½ pound), peeled and thinly sliced , about ⅛ inch thick

3 ounces soft goat cheese (optional)

Preheat the oven to 350 degrees F.

In a large sauté pan, heat the oil over medium-high heat and add the onion. Cook until the onion just begins to brown, 6 to 8 minutes. Add the sausage and cook until the sausage is browned and the onion is soft and velvety, another 10 to 15 minutes. Remove the pan from the heat and allow the sausage to cool completely.

To prepare the phyllo, in a small pan, melt the butter over low heat. You don't want to brown the butter at all. Set the phyllo sheets on the counter and cover with a damp cloth. Working with 1 sheet at a time, use a pastry brush to cover the entire sheet with butter. Put a second sheet of phyllo over the first, and repeat—brushing a thin layer of butter over the entire sheet. Continue working in this way until you have 5 sheets stacked together.

Lightly brush the bottom of a deep 9-inch pie pan with butter and lay the stack of phyllo across the pan. The edges of the phyllo will hang over the sides. Layer the remaining 5 phyllo sheets in this fashion, brushing with melted butter as before. Rotate the pie pan 90 degrees, and lay the second phyllo stack across the pan, perpendicular to the first layer.

Add the first layer of beets to the phyllo, overlapping the edges slightly and covering the bottom. Repeat with half of the apple slices to create a layer over the beets. Season with salt and pepper. Now add a layer of turnips. Over the turnips add half of the sausage mixture.

Continue in this fashion to make another layer of beets, apples, and turnips.

When the last turnip layer is completed, press the filling down hard with your hands, making sure there are no big air pockets or spaces. Add the remaining sausage mixture to the top. If you're using the goat cheese, break it into small pieces and dot over the top of the sausage.

Working clockwise, fold in the corners of the phyllo, creating a pleated top to your pie. Bake until the phyllo is golden brown, 45 to 50 minutes. Let the pie cool for 15 minutes before serving.

apple-stuffed pork loin

Serves 4 to 6

This is a recipe everyone will love. Lean pork loin is butterflied open and stuffed with a bread crumb and apple mixture that is heavy on spices and delivers on flavor. Butterflying the pork loin is easier than you think, so give it a whirl—but if you're not feeling confident, ask the butcher to cut it for you. And don't forget to pick up some kitchen twine while at the grocery store—you will need to tie up this stuffed package before roasting. Pork loin is an affordable cut of meat, as well, which makes this recipe a good one for feeding a crowd. Serve the roast pork with the Apple Pear Salsa with Cilantro (see p. 133) for a fresh-tasting garnish and the Apple Fennel Gratin (see p. 36) as a side dish.

SUGGESTED VARIETIES: *Apples that maintain their flavor with cooking are best. Try Jonagold, Pink Lady, or Sonata.*

STUFFING

2 tablespoons unsalted butter

1 tablespoon olive oil

1 medium yellow onion, finely diced

½ pound cremini mushrooms, finely diced

2 medium apples, cored, and finely diced

1 cup bread crumbs

PORK

1½ pounds boneless pork loin, butterflied

½ teaspoon salt

¼ teaspoon freshly ground pepper

1 tablespoon ground cumin

1 tablespoon ground coriander

2 tablespoons unsalted butter

1 tablespoon olive oil

Preheat the oven to 350 degrees F.

To prepare the stuffing: Add the butter and olive oil to a large sauté pan. When the butter is melted, add the onion and a pinch of salt. Sauté until the onion is soft and translucent, 6 to 8 minutes. Add the mushrooms and stir to coat. The mushrooms will first absorb and then release liquids into the pan. If the pan gets too dry, add 1 or 2 more tablespoons butter. Add the apples and cook until they are softened and begin sticking to the bottom of the pan, 6 to 8 minutes. Immediately add the bread crumbs to the pan, moving it constantly to toast them. When all of the oil is absorbed and the bread crumbs are golden, transfer the stuffing to a plate to cool completely.

To prepare the pork: Lay out the butterflied meat flat on the countertop. Pound out slightly until it is an even thickness. Season the meat with the salt and pepper. Spread a layer of cooled stuffing evenly over the pork loin, an inch from the edges on all sides. Gently roll the pork loin into a thick roll. Stuffing will push out toward the edges. Tie tightly with kitchen twine, securing the roll closed. Scoop up any stuffing that has fallen out and stuff it back into the pork loin.

Sprinkle the cumin and coriander over on the outside of the rolled pork loin until it's well coated. In a large ovenproof sauté pan, heat the butter and olive oil. When the butter has melted, add the rolled pork loin and sear until it's a deep brown on all sides, about 5 minutes total. Put the pan in the oven and roast until the pork is cooked through, about 1 to 1¼ hours or until the meat reaches 150 degrees F on a meat thermometer. Let rest for 10 minutes before serving.

To serve, place the pork on a cutting board and use a serrated knife to cut into thick slices.

lemon-roasted chicken with caramelized onions & apples

Serves 4

This is a perfect roast chicken dish made absolutely fabulous by strategic roasting. Setting the oven at a high temperature to start ensures über-crispy skin and moist meat, while placing the onions and apples on the pan in a single layer and taking care to leave space, results in a perfectly roasted counterpart to the chicken. Those little air pockets create heat traps that brown and char both the onions and apples in the rendered chicken fat, making them irresistible.

SUGGESTED VARIETIES: *Any apple that can hold up to the heat without breaking down is preferred here. Try Pink Lady, Golden Delicious, or Braeburn.*

---

1 teaspoon salt

½ teaspoon freshly ground pepper

Zest from 1 lemon

6 tablespoons chopped fresh thyme, plus more for garnish

One 4- to 5-pound whole chicken, cut into pieces

2 yellow onions, cut into 1-inch dice

2 medium apples, cut into 1-inch dice

In a large bowl, add the salt, pepper, lemon zest, and thyme. Add the chicken, toss to combine, and let marinate on the counter for at least 1 hour before cooking. You can also hold the chicken in the fridge for up to a day.

Preheat the oven to 450 degrees F.

Put the onions and apples on a large rimmed sheet pan, spreading them into a single layer and leaving space between them. Place the seasoned chicken pieces directly on top of the onions and apples, making sure they do not touch or overlap.

Put the sheet pan in the oven and roast for 30 minutes. Without opening the oven door, reduce the heat to 350 degrees F and bake for another 30 to 45 minutes, until the chicken is golden brown and crisp. After the chicken has been roasting for 45 minutes, check the pan every 15 minutes through the oven door; if the onions along the edges are turning too dark, stir as needed (moving the dark onions to the center of the pan, where the heat is cooler) and redistribute the chicken pieces into a single layer before returning to the oven.

After it's finished cooking let the chicken rest for 10 minutes. Transfer the chicken pieces to a serving platter and then spoon on the onions and apples, scraping up all of the brown bits. Garnish with a pinch of fresh thyme if desired. Serve immediately.

DRIED APPLE CHRISTMAS STARS

When my niece Jaclyn was in second grade, her class made Dried Apple Christmas Stars for the tree. The kids dehydrated them by setting the pan on top of the school's radiators, but you can dry out apple slices in the oven. Apples are soaked in citrus and salt to draw out extra moisture and then slowly dehydrated to a crisp. Working in this fashion assures that the slices will not curl along the edges, instead remaining flat and maintaining their natural shape. Thin slivers of apples are baked into curved disks, highlighting the natural star shape in the core. Red Delicious produce the best-shapes, as they have a natural heart shape and a strong star-shaped core.

1 cup lemon juice

1 tablespoon salt

8 Red Delicious apples

Needle

Thread or kitchen twine for hanging

Glue gun for shaping into a wreath (optional)

One 10–12-inch diameter pre-cut wreath-shaped cardboard (optional)

In a large mixing bowl, combine the lemon juice and salt, stirring until all of the salt is dissolved. Set aside.

Using a mandoline or knife, slice the apples horizontally, about ¼ inch thick. (If you prefer a heart-shaped ornament, slice the apples vertically.) Add the apple slices to the lemon juice and steep until the apples absorb the liquid slightly, about 15 minutes.

Preheat the oven to 175 degrees F or its lowest setting. Remove the apple slices from the lemon juice and pat dry with paper towels. Transfer the slices to a parchment-lined baking sheet or to a cooling rack set over a baking sheet and put in the oven.

Bake the apple slices for 6 to 8 hours, turning them every hour to prevent curling. If you don't want your apples to brown, keep the oven door slightly ajar while baking. (You can do this by wedging a stainless-steel spoon between the top of the door and your stovetop.) The apples are done when they are dry to the touch and crisp, but firm. Let them cool completely before continuing.

To make ornaments, use a thin needle with thread to pierce the top of an apple slice, tying a loophole for hanging. You may also weave the thread through the center of the apple star.

To make a wreath, glue apple slices directly onto the cardboard wreath, overlapping the edges slightly.

hard-cider-braised short ribs with apple slaw

Serves 4 to 6

Short ribs are a secondary cut of meat, and one that requires long and slow cooking. The dedication of your time, however, pays off with succulent, fall-off-the-bone meat. These short ribs are braised in a hard apple cider, allowing an apple flavor to shine through without the overt sweetness you expect from apple juice. Typical braising vegetables are added for flavor and pulled from the braising liquid early, so they roast and crisp up in the hot oven as the short ribs finish. If you can't find short ribs, go with a cut of chuck roast, which works equally well.

SUGGESTED VARIETIES: *Apple slaw is best with crisp and tart apples, to complement the braised meat. Try Cameo, Pink Lady, or Granny Smith.*

---

2 pounds beef short ribs

Salt and freshly ground pepper

3 tablespoons olive oil, divided

1 large onion, cut into large chunks

2 medium carrots, peeled and cut into 2-inch pieces

2 celery stalks, cut into 2-inch pieces

22-ounce bottle hard apple cider, divided

1 bay leaf

1 stem fresh rosemary

3 sprigs fresh thyme

APPLE SLAW:

1 medium apple, cored and julienned

3 tablespoons chopped fresh basil

1 teaspoon fresh lime juice

Salt and freshly ground pepper

Liberally salt and pepper the short ribs and set them aside for at least 30 minutes or overnight.

Preheat the oven to 325 degrees F.

In a large Dutch oven or ovenproof sauté pot, add 2 tablespoons of the olive oil and set over medium-high heat. When the oil is hot and rippling, add the short ribs, making sure all of the ribs are touching the bottom of the pot. (Do not stack the ribs.) Brown for 2 minutes, then turn each rib over to brown the other side. Continue working in this fashion until all sides are browned. Remove the short ribs from the pot, reserving them on a plate.

Reduce the heat to medium and adding the onion, carrots, and celery. Cook, stirring often, until the vegetables begin to brown and stick to the bottom of the pot, about 5 minutes. Deglaze the pot with half of the hard apple cider, stirring the bottom to scrape up all the brown bits. The cider will foam up, which is okay. Return the ribs to the pot, nestling them in with the vegetables so they are on the bottom. Add the remaining hard apple cider, the bay leaf, rosemary, and thyme; the cider should cover the ribs fully. If not, add a cup or two of water to cover.

Bring to a boil, then cover the pot and put it in the oven. Bake until the meat falls off the bone and shreds easily with a fork, about 3 hours. While the ribs are braising, check them every 30 minutes or so to be sure the braising liquid doesn't evaporate; replace with stock or water as needed. You want the ribs to be just covered in liquid at all times.

After 2½ hours, remove the pot from the oven and strain out the vegetables using a slotted spoon, draining off the stock. Drain well or the vegetables will not brown. Transfer the vegetables to a roasting pan in a single layer, and add the remaining tablespoon of olive oil, stirring to coat. Replace the pot in the oven along with the vegetable pan; roast until the vegetables are crisp and brown, about 30 minutes.

To prepare the slaw: Put the apple in a small bowl and toss with the basil, lime juice, and a pinch of salt and pepper. Stir to combine and adjust the salt as needed. Set aside until you're ready to serve.

Remove the roasted vegetables and short ribs from the oven. Place the short ribs in the center of a serving platter and position the roasted vegetables around them. Set the pot on the stovetop over high heat. Boil, reducing the liquid down to a gravy, for 12 to 15 minutes, or until the consistency is to your liking. Strain the gravy and pour over the ribs. Sprinkle apple slaw over the ribs and serve immediately.

CELLARING APPLES

Cellaring fruit and vegetables is the historical practice of holding produce in an underground chamber in order to prolong its shelf life. Basements, underground caves, and even a box full of sand kept in an unheated but insulated garage can act as a root cellar. Keeping apples in a cellar slows ripening of fruit and inhibits the process of decay. In winter, cellars will help keep apples from freezing, which prevents spoilage.

Apples properly stored in a cellar may keep for up to 3 months, making them strong candidates for buying in bulk during fall and holding in cold storage. To store apples, wrap each individual apple in black-and-white newspaper. Choose apples that are perfect; steer clear of any with cuts or bruises. Wrapping apples carefully protects them from touching. This is an important step, prohibiting any rotting apples from ruining the whole box. Stack apples in a dry cardboard box, placing varieties that keep best toward the bottom. Tart apples with thick skins make for good storing apples, though you should talk to a local farmer for advice.

pies, crumbles & cakes

vanilla-caramel poached apple halves with mascarpone

Serves 6

This dessert is a perfect make-ahead recipe to serve after a heavy autumnal meal. You make a quick batch of caramelized sugar before melting it into a portion of water. This caramel-like water is then used to just poach the apple halves. For entertaining, you can make these apples a day ahead and hold them in the fridge overnight with good results.

SUGGESTED VARIETIES: *Any apple that can hold up to the heat without breaking down is preferred here. Try Pink Lady, Golden Delicious, or Braeburn.*

2¼ cups sugar

5½ cups warm water

1 whole vanilla bean pod, split, seeds
  reserved

4 small apples

¼ cup mascarpone

In a large dry saucepan, add the sugar and shake, gently, so it forms an even layer along the bottom. Set the pan over medium-high heat and do not stir the sugar, but monitor it closely. It will begin to brown at the edges. Swirl the pan slightly to distribute the heat and hot caramel, making sure to keep the sugar level so it does not coat the sides of the saucepan. The caramel will turn dark brown and amber at the edges. Continue swirling gently until all of the sugar is dark amber, 5 to 7 minutes. Pour in the warm water and stir. Be careful, because the caramelized sugar will sputter and pop. Cook until the caramelized sugar has dissolved, add the vanilla bean pod, remove the pan from the heat, and set aside.

Peel the apples, leaving their stems intact. Cut them in half lengthwise, scoop out their cores with a small spoon, and immediately drop them into the syrup. When all of the apples have been added to the syrup, return the pan to medium-high heat. Bring to a low boil, then reduce the heat to medium-low. Cook the apples until they are just soft, 20 to 30 minutes. Check for doneness by piercing with a paring knife: A cooked apple will be easily pierced, but still offer slight resistance near the center. Remove the pan from the heat and set aside to cool.

In a small bowl, stir together the mascarpone and reserved vanilla seeds until combined. To serve, use a slotted spoon to remove each apple half from the syrup and place in a shallow bowl. Add a dollop of vanilla mascarpone to the hollowed center, pour a spoonful of the caramel poaching liquid into the bowl, and serve.

carrot-apple cake with citrus cream cheese frosting

Serves 6

This cake is heavy with apples and carrots, resulting in an ultra-moist, custard-like cake crumb. The density of the fruit really pulls on the cake batter, so this is not a traditional fluffy cake, and will actually collapse a bit when cooling. No matter, though, as it allows for a shallow pocket that you can fill with citrus-scented icing.

SUGGESTED VARIETIES: *A strong-flavored apple works well here, allowing the apple-y note to shine through. Try Granny Smith, Idared, or Sonata.*

CAKE

1 cup granulated sugar

1 cup brown sugar

½ cup (1 stick) unsalted butter, at room temperature

½ cup plain yogurt

3 large eggs

1 tablespoon vanilla extract

1 tablespoon grated fresh gingerroot

2 cups all-purpose flour

1 teaspoon baking powder

1 teaspoon baking soda

1 teaspoon salt

1 teaspoon ground cinnamon

2 large carrots, peeled and grated

2 medium apples, cored and grated

ICING

8 ounces cream cheese, at room temperature

½ cup powdered sugar

½ cup plain yogurt

½ teaspoon grated fresh gingerroot

Zest from 1 orange

Preheat the oven to 350 degrees F.

Grease a 9-inch cake pan with a removable bottom (or a 9-inch springform pan) and line with parchment. Set aside.

To prepare the cake: In the bowl of an electric mixer, cream the sugars and butter on medium-high speed until light and fluffy, about 5 minutes. Add the yogurt and blend until just mixed, being sure to scrape down the sides of the bowl. Add the eggs one at a time, mixing until well incorporated, making sure to scrape the sides of the bowl between each addition. Add the vanilla and ginger and stir to combine.

In a medium bowl, combine all of the dry ingredients and mix well. Add the dry ingredients to the wet mixture and stir until just combined. Add the grated carrots and apples and stir on low speed until evenly incorporated.

Pour the batter into the prepared pan and bake for about 60 minutes, until a knife inserted into the cake comes out free of batter. Let the cake cool for 15 to 20 minutes before removing the cake from the pan by pressing up on the bottom. If the cake does not release easily, run a butter knife along the edges of the cake pan to loosen.

To prepare the icing: While the cake is baking, add the cream cheese to a medium bowl and beat to soften. Sift in the powdered sugar and stir with a flat rubber spatula to incorporate completely. Add the yogurt, ginger, and orange zest. Stir until the icing is smooth and has no lumps, then chill until you're ready to use it.

Allow the cream cheese frosting to warm up a little if it's been in the fridge, so you can spread it more easily.

Add a generous dollop to the center of the cake. Using an offset spatula or butter knife, spread the icing out just to the edges, allowing it to pool a little on top. Any leftover cake should be stored in the fridge, lightly wrapped in plastic wrap, where it will keep for several days.

DIY APPLE JUICE

Making apple juice at home is a fairly easy task that requires no special equipment and results in a juice smacking of fresh apple flavor that you'd be hard-pressed to find elsewhere. (Get it, pressed?) During apple season, buy apples in bulk and plan to use them in a variety of ways. Buying in bulk assures a lower price and allows you to stock up on apple products for the year—apple butter, cider vinegar, and juice are all excellent methods for extending the season.

Apples produce a vast amount of juice. This juice is easily extracted through the process of slow-steaming. A large pot is filled with roughly chopped apple pieces and a low level of water and brought to a simmer. This process of cooking out the apples slowly allows the fruits to release their juice, eventually filling the pot.

Homemade apple juice will lack the clarity of store-bought juices, but this cloudiness can be attributed to fruit fibers and pectin left behind—both excellent sources of nutrition. For a more clear juice, the liquid can be strained through cheesecloth several times. Mix and match your apple varieties, guaranteeing a well-rounded juice. Work to balance sweet apples with tart apples, resulting in a perfect glass of juice.

HOMEMADE APPLE JUICE

Makes 8 quarts

20 pounds apples, cored and cut into large pieces

1 cup sugar (optional)

Add 4 inches of water to a very large pot (or several). Fill the pot with apple pieces almost to the top. Set the pot over high heat and bring it to a boil, then reduce it to a simmer and leave the apples to steam, occasionally pressing down on the apple solids to help release their juice. Steam the apples until they're completely soft and the pot is nearly full with juice, anywhere from 1 to 2 hours.

To filter the juice, set up a fine-mesh strainer over a large bowl and ladle out the apple mash and liquid, working in batches. (Reserve the mash for applesauce, or for cider vinegar starter.) If you would like a clearer liquid, set up a fine-mesh strainer and line it with 4 layers of moistened cheesecloth. Working in batches, pour the apple juice over the cheesecloth and let it drain into bowl below. This can be done several times, using a thicker layer of cheesecloth if desired.

Taste the juice for sweetness, adding as much or as little sugar as you like. Stir until completely dissolved.

Add the apple juice to clean, sterilized canning jars, leaving 1 inch head space. Using a damp clean towel, wipe the rims of the jars, and top them with lids and rings. Process in a water bath for 10 minutes. Remove each jar with tongs and let them cool on the counter. Once they're cool, make sure the seals are secure. Sealed jars may be stored in a cool, dark cupboard for up to 1 year. The other method is freezing—fill plastic containers or gallon-size resealable plastic bags and store in the freezer.

upside-down apple tart

Serves 4

This apple tart comes together quickly and is an easy dessert for last-minute meals or tossing together on a busy day. You start by melting sugar in a hot pan—effectively a quick caramel sauce. From there, you need only lay out apple slices and cover them with a disk of store-bought puff pastry before baking. The caramel browns up the apples in a decadent sauce, and the pastry puffs up flaky and golden brown. I always mix and match my apples, layering the flavor, but if you only have one variety, opt for baking apples, which tend to hold their shape and will release from the pan more readily.

SUGGESTED VARIETIES: *Try tart apples that maintain their flavor, such as Granny Smith, Pippin, or Cortland.*

---

1 sheet puff pastry, thawed	¼ teaspoon ground cinnamon
3 medium apples, thinly sliced	½ lemon, juiced
¼ teaspoon ground nutmeg	⅓ cup plus 2 tablespoons sugar

Lay the sheet of puff pastry on the countertop and roll it out slightly, to ⅛-inch thickness. Place a large ovenproof sauté pan (about 8 inches in diameter) over the sheet and cut out a circle of pastry to fit. Set aside. Save any leftover pastry for another use.

In a large mixing bowl, toss the apple slices with the spices, lemon juice, and 2 tablespoons of the sugar. Set aside.

Preheat the oven to 350 degrees F.

In the sauté pan, add the remaining ⅓ cup sugar and shake gently so it forms an even layer along the bottom. Set the pan over medium-high heat; the sugar will start melting after a few moments. Swirl the pan slightly to distribute the heat and hot caramel, making sure not to let it burn in places. When the caramel is a golden brown, immediately remove the pan from the heat.

Add the apple slices to the pan, laying them in a neat circle. The apples will sizzle slightly in the hot caramel. Start along the outside edge and work your way in, overlapping each layer slightly, until you reach the center of the pan. Place the puff pastry disk over the apples and tuck the edges in and under with the tip of a paring knife. Bake for about 30 minutes or until the pastry is a deep golden brown.

Remove the tart from the pan immediately. To release the tart, cover the sauté pan with an inverted large plate and hold tightly. Flip over and lift off pan. The tart should release onto the plate easily when hot. If the caramel cools and sticks, put the sauté pan over a burner on low heat to melt and loosen before you try inverting it again.

Serve immediately with vanilla ice cream or sweetened whipped cream.

whole wheat apple & yogurt cake

Serves 6

Baking an apple cake on a weekend morning is an indulgence that instantly fills the house with enticing smells. This cake is made with whole wheat flour and yogurt, so it is dense and wholesome. Apples are chopped and layered inside the cake and sprinkled along the cake bottom, creating a caramelly and crisp slice. I use a Bundt pan in this recipe, but feel free to opt for a 9-inch cake pan instead.

SUGGESTED VARIETIES: *Any baking apple will do. Try Rome, Braeburn, or Winesap.*

STREUSEL

½ cup brown sugar

¼ cup granulated sugar

¼ cup all-purpose flour

¼ teaspoon ground cloves

Pinch of salt

¼ cup (½ stick) unsalted butter, chilled and cut into small cubes

CAKE

2 large apples, cored and diced

½ cup brown sugar

1 tablespoon ground cinnamon

1¼ cups all-purpose flour

1¼ cups whole wheat flour

1 teaspoon baking soda

1 teaspoon baking powder

¼ teaspoon salt

½ cup (1 stick) unsalted butter, softened

1 cup granulated sugar

3 large eggs

1½ cups plain yogurt

1 tablespoon vanilla extract

Preheat the oven to 350 degrees F. Butter a Bundt pan well, being sure to coat the creases. Set aside.

To prepare the streusel: Put the sugars, flour, cloves, and salt in a medium bowl and stir to combine. Cut the butter using your fingertips. Massage the mixture together until it forms a coarse crumb and set aside.

To prepare the cake: In a medium bowl, add the apples, brown sugar, and cinnamon, and stir very well to combine. Set aside.

In another medium bowl, add the flours, baking soda, baking powder, and salt. Stir to combine thoroughly and set aside.

In the bowl of an electric mixer, cream together the butter and sugar on medium-high speed until light and fluffy, about 5 minutes. Scrape down the sides of the bowl, if necessary. Add the eggs one at a time, mixing until well incorporated, making sure to scrape the sides of the bowl between each addition.

Once the eggs are blended fully, add half of the dry ingredients and mix until well combined, about 1 minute. Pour in the yogurt and vanilla and mix briefly, until just combined. Add the remaining dry ingredients and mix until incorporated. These last 2 steps should take about 1 minute total.

Pour half of the batter into the Bundt pan, distributing evenly around the circle. Sprinkle about two thirds of the apple mixture over the batter. Fill the Bundt pan with the remaining batter, covering the apples completely. Layer the rest of the apple mixture over the batter and sprinkle the streusel topping over the entire cake bottom. Bake for 50 to 60 minutes, until a knife inserted into the cake comes out clean.

Let the cake cool for 15 to 20 minutes before turning the Bundt pan over onto a plate and loosening the cake to serve. Leftover cake can be kept at room temperature wrapped tightly in plastic for several days.

apple almond tart

Makes 1 tart; serves 6 to 8

I love the simplicity of a baked tart made in a fluted tart pan. The pretty scalloped edge is gorgeous when brown and crisp, and its shallow nature allows for the perfect bit of sweetness to end a meal. The nut filling bakes down to a slightly chewy, dense consistency that is perked up by the softened fruit. You can use pistachios instead of almonds, and still produce excellent results. Be sure to slice your apples thinly for this tart, and lay them in an organized circular pattern. The edges will darken and crisp, and the tart will look gorgeous when served whole and cut at the table.

SUGGESTED VARIETIES: *Choose apple-y apples, like Golden Delicious, Rome, or Granny Smith.*

TART DOUGH

½ cup all-purpose flour

½ cup whole wheat pastry flour

½ teaspoon salt

½ teaspoon sugar

½ cup (1 stick) unsalted butter, chilled and cut into small cubes

¼ cup ice water, plus more if needed

FILLING

½ cup (1 stick) unsalted butter, at room temperature

½ cup granulated sugar

1 large egg

1 egg yolk

1 teaspoon vanilla extract

1 cup whole almonds, toasted, cooled, and finely ground

2 teaspoons all-purpose flour

¼ teaspoon salt

2 medium apples, cored and thinly sliced (about ¼ inch)

1 tablespoon demerara sugar

To make the tart dough, combine all of the dry ingredients in the bowl of a food processor, and pulse once or twice to combine. Add the butter cubes to the bowl. Pulse until the dough forms into large crumbles, being careful not to overmix, about 30 pulses. Add the ice water to the bowl and turn the processor on, mixing until the dough is just combined and comes together in 2 or 3 large portions. This only takes about 8 to 10 seconds, so be mindful not to overprocess. Turn the dough out onto the countertop and press into a flat round disk (about 6 inches wide). Work quickly and don't handle the dough too much. Wrap it tightly in plastic wrap and chill for at least 2 hours, or until you're ready to roll it out.

Lightly flour a work surface and roll out the dough into a 10-inch round, making sure to rotate and flip it over, rolling both sides. Fold it in half loosely and place it over a 9-inch tart pan with a removable bottom, the crease of the dough running down the middle of the pan, and the edges overhanging slightly. Unfold the dough so it hangs over the edge of the tart pan. Press the dough gently into the corners of the pan, being careful not to stretch it thin. Fold under any overhanging crust, and press it into the walls of tart pan. Run a rolling pin over the top of the pan, pressing down to trim any extra dough and make it flush with top edge of the pan. Use a fork to pierce the bottom of the tart shell, and freeze for 30 minutes.

Preheat the oven to 350 degrees F. Take the tart shell from the freezer and line it with parchment paper. Fill the parchment paper with pie weights or beans, pressing them into the corners. Bake for 20 minutes. Remove the pie weights and bake for another 10 to 15 minutes, until golden brown. Remove the shell from the oven and cool for at least 15 minutes, or until you're ready to use it.

To prepare the filling: When you're ready to make the filling, be sure the oven is preheated to 350 degrees F. In the bowl of an electric mixer, cream together the butter and sugar until fluffy and white, about 5 minutes. Add the egg, egg yolk, and vanilla, and mix well to combine. Add the ground almonds, flour, and salt; mix together until well combined.

Spread the filling into the pre-baked tart shell. Press the apple slices into the almond filling, slightly overlapping them and working in a circle from the outside of the tart to the center. Sprinkle with the demerara sugar and bake until the apples are golden brown, 40 to 45 minutes. Cool before serving.

apple-pear crisp

Serves 4 to 6

Crisps come together quickly and easily and always produce excellent results. Topped with a crispy and addictive crumb topping, this baked fruit dish is as indispensable as it is flexible. For this crisp, apples and pears work together to produce a well-rounded natural sweetness, cutting down on the need for additional sugar. Almond meal gives the crisp topping a toothsome bite while the nuttiness complements the baked fruit below. Feel free to double up on the almond meal in place of the flour for a gluten-free version that everyone will love.

SUGGESTED VARIETIES: *Choose and firm, crisp apples, like Golden Delicious, Rome, or Cortland, and blend with a soft apple such as McIntosh for texture.*

FRUIT

3 to 5 medium apples, cored and cut into
   1-inch pieces

3 medium Bosc pears, cored and cut into
   2-inch pieces

¼ cup sugar

¼ teaspoon ground cloves

CRISP

½ cup almond meal

¾ cup rolled oats

½ cup brown sugar

1½ teaspoons ground cinnamon

¼ teaspoon freshly ground nutmeg

¼ teaspoon salt

6 tablespoons (¾ stick) unsalted butter,
   chilled and cut into small pieces

Preheat the oven to 350 degrees F.

To prepare the fruit: Add the apples and pears to a large mixing bowl. Sprinkle with the sugar and cloves, and stir to combine. Pour the fruit along with any juices into a deep 8-inch square baking pan and set aside.

To prepare the crisp: Using the same mixing bowl, add the almond meal, oats, sugar, spices, and salt; stir to combine. Add the butter to the bowl. Using your fingers, pinch the butter into the dry ingredients, blending well. The topping will at first resemble coarse crumbs, but will soon come together in larger clumps.

Distribute the topping evenly over the fruit in the pan, breaking up larger clumps if needed. Bake for 40 to 45 minutes, until the fruit can be easily pierced with a fork and the crisp topping is golden brown. Let the crisp cool for 15 minutes before serving. Serve with a scoop of vanilla ice cream or a dollop of whipped cream.

apple strudel

Serves 8

This apple strudel steers clear of the traditional hand-pulled dough, and instead takes a shortcut with store-bought puff pastry. Thin, buttery dough puffs up in the oven when cooked and envelops a soft apple filling spiked simply with cinnamon and sugar. This works as both a fancy morning pastry and an after-dinner sweet, particularly when paired with a scoop of vanilla ice cream.

SUGGESTED VARIETIES: *Choose any baking apple you like for this strudel. Cortland, Macoun, and Winesap work well together.*

¼ cup raisins (optional)

2 tablespoons rum (optional)

2 tablespoons ground cinnamon

½ cup sugar

4 to 5 medium apples, cored, peeled, and thinly sliced

2 sheets (1 package) puff pastry, thawed

All-purpose flour, for dusting

2 tablespoons unsalted butter, melted

Preheat the oven to 375 degrees F.

In a small bowl, add the raisins and rum, if using. Let the raisins soak in and absorb the rum.

While the raisins are soaking, combine the cinnamon and sugar in another small bowl. In a large bowl, combine the apples with half of the cinnamon-sugar mixture, tossing to coat evenly. Set aside.

Lightly flour the countertop and set out 1 sheet of puff pastry. Dust the top lightly with flour and roll it out, keeping the rectangular shape, until the dough is about ¼ inch thick. Sprinkle half of the remaining cinnamon-sugar mixture over the entire pastry. Spread half of the apple mixture along the length of the pastry, stacking the slices slightly, leaving a 1-inch border from the edge. Sprinkle with half the raisins, if using. Fold the pastry edge up and over the apples, and then—using both hands to hold the apples firmly in place—roll the strudel, covering the apples completely. Pinch together the ends and tuck them under to seal. Working quickly, lift the strudel and set it on a baking sheet. Working in the same fashion, shape the second pastry, sprinkle with the last of the cinnamon-sugar, fill with apples and raisins, and fold, shaping into a strudel. Place the second strudel on the baking sheet.

Using a sharp knife, make several cuts across the tops of the strudels. Brush both strudels with the melted butter and bake in the oven until puffed up and golden brown, 35 to 45 minutes. Let cool before serving.

traditional apple pie

Makes one 9-inch pie

My brother swears by his recipe for apple pie, but I'm pretty sure I have him beat. He relies on shortening to introduce flakiness to the dough, while I prefer an all-butter crust. The secret to amazing pie dough is working quickly and being careful not to overprocess. Leaving big chunks of butter in the dough will allow for a light, flaky crust—as the butter melts, it will leave behind tender air pockets that layer the dough, making way for a crispy, delicate shell. As for the apples, I tend to mix and match, never committing solely to one variety.

SUGGESTED VARIETIES: *Baking apples are meant for pie! Try Spitzenburg, Gravenstein, or Bramley's Seedling, which are all heirloom varieties and can likely be found at your local farmer's market. If you can't find heirloom apples, Granny Smith and McIntosh are excellent pie apples.*

DOUGH

2½ cups all-purpose flour

1 teaspoon salt

1 teaspoon sugar

1 cup (2 sticks) unsalted butter, chilled and cut into small cubes

½ cup ice-cold water

FILLING

6 medium apples (about 2½ pounds), cored and sliced into ½-inch wedges

⅔ cup brown sugar

3 tablespoons all-purpose flour

1 tablespoon grated fresh orange zest

½ teaspoon ground cinnamon

½ teaspoon ground nutmeg

¼ teaspoon salt

To prepare the dough, put all of the dry ingredients into a food processor, and pulse once or twice to combine. Add the butter and pulse just until the dough forms large crumbles—be careful not to overmix. (Typically, I pulse between 30 and 38 times.) Pour in the ice water and pulse until just combined and the dough starts to come together in 2 or 3 large portions. This takes 8 to 10 seconds, so be mindful not to overprocess.

Turn the dough out onto the countertop and divide in half, pressing each half into a flat round disks about 6 inches in diameter. Be careful not to overwork the dough. Wrap each piece tightly in plastic wrap and refrigerate for at least 2 hours before rolling out.

To prepare the filling: While the dough is chilling put all of the filling ingredients in a large bowl and stir to combine well. Set aside.

When the dough has chilled, remove 1 dough disk from the fridge and preheat the oven to 350 degrees F. Lightly flour a work surface. Using a rolling pin, roll out the dough into about an 11-inch round (be sure to rotate the dough and flip it over, rolling both sides). Keep your work surface lightly floured so the dough does not stick.

Fold the round in half loosely and place it over a 9-inch pie pan (the crease of the dough should run down the middle of the pan). Unfold the dough so it hangs over the edge of the pan. Press it gently into the sides of the pan, being careful not to stretch it too thin, letting the dough hang over the sides. Pierce the bottom of the pie shell with a fork in several places. Put in the freezer while you roll the second disk in the same fashion.

When the second disk has been rolled out, remove the pie pan from the freezer and fill with the apple filling, mounding slightly in the center. Fold the second rolled disk in half loosely and place over the top of the apples. The crease of the dough should run down the middle of the apples. Unfold the dough so it hangs over the edge of the pie pan.

Using a knife or kitchen shears, trim the dough edges so that they are just about flush with the edge of the pie pan. Press the edges together lightly and crimp with your fingers, creating a scalloped edge. Cut several steam vents in the top of the dough. I will often make slits in the center, creating a star, or carve in someone's initials or the date for any special occasion.

Put the pie on the center rack of the oven and bake until golden brown, 60 to 75 minutes. If the top or edges of the pie begin to crisp and burn, wrap them loosely with a ring of foil and/or cover the top of the pie with a sheet of foil.

Let the pie cool for at least 1 hour before serving.

apple cider doughnuts

Makes 36 small doughnuts

Doughnuts need not be a labor of love, and these simple drop doughnuts prove just that with their simplicity. Apple cider is boiled and reduced down to concentrate the flavor, while yogurt is added to a yeasted dough for a bit of tang. The sour-sweet combination makes for a super-tasty doughnut that can be shaken with powdered sugar or a cinnamon-sugar. For a light and fluffy doughnut, make sure you don't overmix the batter, which will stimulate the gluten in the flour and create a tougher texture.

---

5 cups all-purpose flour

3 tablespoons baking powder

1 teaspoon ground cinnamon

1 teaspoon ground nutmeg

1 tablespoon salt

½ cup (1 stick) unsalted butter, at room temperature

1 cup granulated sugar

3 large eggs

½ cup plain yogurt

1 tablespoon vanilla extract

2 cups apple cider, boiled until reduced by half (1 cup total)

Vegetable oil, for frying

1 cup powdered sugar *or* 1 cup granulated sugar plus 1 teaspoon ground cinnamon, for serving

---

In a medium bowl, add the flour, baking powder, cinnamon, nutmeg, and salt. Stir to combine thoroughly and set aside.

In the bowl of an electric mixer, cream the butter and sugar on medium-high speed until light and fluffy, about 5 minutes. Scrape down the sides of the bowl, if necessary. Add the eggs one at a time, mixing until well incorporated, making sure to scrape the sides of the bowl between each addition.

Once the eggs are blended fully, add half of the dry ingredients and mix until well combined, about 1 minute. Pour in the yogurt and vanilla and mix briefly, until just combined. Add the remainder of the dry ingredients and mix until incorporated. These last 2 steps should take 1 minute total.

Add the reduced apple cider to the bowl and mix until just combined—there may be a few lumps. Cover the surface of the dough with a layer of plastic wrap and refrigerate until cold, 2 to 3 hours.

Turn the dough out onto a floured countertop and knead it briefly to even it out into a soft mound. The dough should be soft with a smooth surface; it won't need much flour incorporated. Pat or roll the dough into a wide rectangular shape about 1½ inches thick. Using a knife, cut the dough into small 2-inch squares.

When you're ready to fry the doughnuts, add about ½ inch of oil to a large sauté pan, and set the pan over medium heat. The oil is ready when it hits 375 degrees F, or a small piece of dough dropped in bubbles quickly and floats. Using a small spatula, drop the doughnuts into the hot oil and fry, being careful not to overcrowd the pan. Cook on one side until golden brown, about 2 minutes, and turn over. Cook the other side until golden brown, another 2 minutes or so. When they're brown, drain the doughnuts on several layers of paper towel or on a paper bag and cool slightly. Once they're cool enough to handle, but still warm, either shake powdered sugar over them or toss in cinnamon-sugar.

Any extra dough can be shaped, cut, and frozen for frying at a later date.

PERFECT PIES

Choosing the right apples for baking the perfect apple pie is a debatable and subjective topic, particularly as more varieties of apple become available.

Aim to choose apples that are both tart and slightly sweet. Apples should maintain their apple-y flavor through baking. A pie that balances the acidity of a tart apple (like Granny Smith) with the sweetness from another variety (Honeycrisp) is a winner. Apples range in flavor, however, even within varieties. Sun, temperature, and harvest time all affect taste, so while one year Orin apples may be perfectly delicious, the next year's harvest may fall flat. It is important that you taste apples before you buy. If you're at a farmers' market, most farms will oblige and cut a sliver for tasting. Ditto in some grocery stores, and it couldn't hurt to ask.

Texture, too, plays a big part in choosing the appropriate pie apple—flesh that holds its shape and allows for a bit of bite in a done pie is preferable. My goal is to bake up a pie with both texture and give, leaving some apples whole while other thin slices break down to near-sauce. Personally, I like a mixture in my pie and refuse to commit to one variety.

Cider apples make for good pie apples as well. Any of the Russets will maintain both their flavor and their shape in a pie. Because cider apples can be more acidic, you may need to adjust the sugar level in the filling. Taste and decide on your own.

Nationally, Braeburn, Golden Delicious, and Granny Smith are widely available, and all will make an excellent start to any pie. Add a Jonathan, Northern Spy, Macoun, Gravenstein, or Winesap and you'll be off to a great start.

fried apple hand pies

Makes 12 to 15 hand pies

The filling for these apple hand pies is heavily spiked with warming spices and cooked down to a thick fragrant syrup. The crust is flaky and layered, and it makes for perfect hand pies. These can be shaped and made ahead, and fried just before serving. It is important that shaped pies are trimmed of any extra dough, and that the dough is kept thin so that it cooks completely in the oil.

SUGGESTED VARIETIES: *Cooking apples are best in this recipe, as they retain their apple flavor and easily break down to a smooth puree. Try Winesap, McIntosh, or Braeburn.*

DOUGH

2½ cups all-purpose flour

1 teaspoon baking soda

¼ teaspoon salt

½ cup (1 stick) unsalted butter, chilled
   and cut into small cubes

1 large egg

5 tablespoons ice-water

FILLING

3 medium apples, cored and chopped into
   ½-inch pieces

½ cup sugar

1 teaspoon ground cinnamon

¼ teaspoon ground cloves

1 teaspoon vanilla extract

¼ cup apple cider (or water)

½ cup vegetable oil

To prepare the dough: Add the flour, baking soda, and salt to a food processor and pulse to combine. Sprinkle the butter evenly over the top of the flour and pulse until the mixture resembles coarse crumbs, about 30 pulses. Combine the egg with the ice water and beat until blended. With the machine running, quickly pour the egg mixture down the feeding tube and process until the dough just comes together into 1 or 2 large balls, about 30 seconds. Turn the dough out onto the countertop. Divide it in half, pressing each half into a flat round disks about 6 inches in diameter. Be careful not to work the dough. Wrap each piece tightly in plastic wrap and refrigerate for at least 2 hours before rolling out.

To prepare the filling: In a medium saucepan, add all of the filling ingredients and set over medium heat. Cook, stirring occasionally, until the apples are soft and the liquid forms a thick syrup. You don't want a watery filling, so you're aiming to evaporate some of the moisture from the pan. You should end up with a thick mass of apples that can be easily mashed with a fork. When the mixture is cooked, remove the pan from the heat and cool completely.

To prepare the apple pies: remove one dough disk from the fridge. Divide the disk into into 6 even pieces. Working with one at a time, roll out into a thin, rectangular sheet, about 5 inches long and 4 inches wide, between 2 sheets of plastic wrap. (Using plastic wrap cuts down on the need for board flour, which dries out this dough.) When all 6 sheets are rolled out, add a heaping spoonful of filling to the bottom half of a rectangle, leaving a bit of spice along the edges. Fold the dough over to form a small rectangular pie and press out the air while sealing the edges together. Using the tines of a fork, crimp the edges, pressing down, which will help thin the dough so you don't end up with thick, uncooked edges. Trim any long dough from the edges—you are aiming for them to be about ½ inch wide.

Once each pie is formed, place it on a sheet pan and hold in the freezer. Keep adding to the sheet pan as you form more pies. Divide the second piece of dough into 6 pieces and repeat the rolling, filling, and folding process. Any extra dough from trimming can be re-rolled and formed into a pie.

When you're ready to fry the pies, add ½ inch of oil to a large sauté pan, and set the pan over medium heat. The oil is ready when it hits 375 degrees F, or a small piece of dough dropped in bubbles quickly and floats. One by one, carefully drop the pies into the oil, making sure not to overcrowd the pan. Cook until the first side is golden brown, about 4 minutes. Turn the pie over and cook the other side until golden brown, another 4 minutes. Remove the pies from the oil and place on a paper bag or layer of paper towels to drain. You can hold the warm pies in the oven or serve them immediately.

whole baked cinnamon-cardamom apples

Serves 6

This recipe is healthy and simple—the perfect dessert for when you're craving something sweet, but can't afford the extra calories. Apples are baked with a bit of spice-heavy butter and served whole. Of course, you can pair these gems with a scoop of vanilla ice cream, but I find them to be super satisfying even without the indulgence.

SUGGESTED VARIETIES: *Apples that hold their shape and are still a bit sweet are best for baking whole for dessert. Try Jonathan, Spitzenburg, or Honeycrisp.*

---

6 medium apples, cored, bottoms left intact

6 tablespoons (¾ stick) unsalted butter, at room temperature

1½ teaspoons ground cinnamon

1½ teaspoons ground cardamom

¼ teaspoon salt

Preheat the oven to 375 degrees F. Place the cored apples snuggly in a shallow baking dish and set aside.

In a small bowl, combine the butter, cinnamon, cardamom, and salt. Using the back of a spoon, mash the mixture together until well combined.

Fill each hollowed apple core with 1 tablespoon of the seasoned butter, packing it down. Bake on the center rack for 40 to 45 minutes until the apples are soft and easily pierced with a knife. Let cool for 15 minutes before serving.

HOMEMADE CARAMEL APPLES

Caramel apples smack of autumn and conjure the excitement and wonderment of Halloween. They are also excellent ways to encourage kids to eat fruit when piles of candy abound. Kids can dip their own caramel apples, but are better left out of the caramel-making process—cooked sugar is very hot and dangerous to work with. Have kids help spearing the apples, and consider setting out a bowl of toppings for dipping hot caramel apples in. Crushed nuts, coconut flakes, and even sprinkles are festive.

Makes 8 apples

8 medium apples

1½ cups sugar

½ cup light corn syrup

½ cup heavy cream, warmed slightly

1 teaspoon vanilla extract

To prepare the apples, insert a Popsicle stick or short, thin branch directly into the center of the core, pressing down firmly to secure.

In a medium saucepan, add the sugar and corn syrup and set over medium-high heat. Cover the pan and cook until the sugar melts, about 7 minutes. Remove the lid and continue cooking the syrup, which will be boiling and climbing up the sides of the pan slightly. Watch the sugar—it will be clear at first. Using a wet pastry brush, wash down the sides of the pan regularly. This prevents crystals from forming and ruining the caramel.

with the
Kids

Swirl the pan occasionally, and cook until the mixture turns from golden to amber, about 10 minutes in total. The liquid will be fragrant. Working quickly, add the warmed heavy cream slowly. Wear an oven mitt and stand back, as the liquid will sputter and pop. Once the boiling has subsided, remove the pan from the heat and pour the caramel into a deep, narrow heat-proof bowl and let it stand for 5 minutes.

Once the caramel has cooled slightly, it will thicken. Stir until the caramel is smooth and without bubbles. Dip the bottom of a test apple into the caramel. If the caramel runs easily off the apple, let it stand for another 5 minutes to thicken. When the caramel is thick enough to work with, dip the apples one at a time, rotating to coat the fruit. Pull the apple from the caramel and swirl gently, allowing the excess caramel to drip back into the bowl. If the caramel hardens while you're working, simply reheat it over a double boiler until it loosens.

Set the dipped apples on a parchment-lined baking sheet to cool and harden. Let kids sprinkle on toppings, if using, while caramel is still warm. They can press it into the sides with their hands or roll the apple in a small plate of topping. Serve when the caramel is completely cool. To store the apples, wrap in a loose layer of parchment paper and close with a portion of kitchen twine. Hold at room temperature until you're ready to serve.

jams, relishes & chutneys

spiced apple chutney

Makes about 6 half-pint jars

Chutneys are savory fruit-based spreads often used in Indian cuisine. Here, apples are perfumed with commanding winter spices. This fragrant chutney has a bit of a heat from red pepper flakes and cayenne pepper. Cider apples make the best chutney, as they are tart and firm and hold their shape after cooking.

SUGGESTED VARIETIES: *If you can't find cider apples, substitute another firm apple like Granny Smith or the English variety Bramley's Seedling.*

---

2 tablespoons olive oil

1 medium yellow onion, finely chopped

1 teaspoon salt

2 pounds cider apples, cored and cut into small dice

12 whole cloves

1 teaspoon ground cinnamon

½ teaspoon curry powder

½ teaspoon ground cardamom

½ teaspoon red pepper flakes

¼ teaspoon ground allspice

¼ teaspoon cayenne pepper

2 teaspoon mustard seeds, coarsely ground

2 tablespoons finely chopped crystallized ginger

½ cup raisins

1 cup apple cider vinegar

½ cup brown sugar

Heat the oil in a large saucepan over medium-high heat. Add the onion and salt and sauté until the onion starts to brown, 10 to 12 minutes. Add the apples and sauté until they start to brown, another 10 to 12 minutes. Add all of the spices, ginger, and raisins, stirring for 2 minutes to incorporate. Add the apple cider vinegar and brown sugar. Bring to a boil and then reduce the heat to a simmer. Cook until the mixture is thick and the apples are very soft but still hold their shape, 45 minutes to 1 hour.

Fill clean, sterilized jars with chutney, leaving ½ inch head space. Using a damp, clean towel, wipe the rims of the jars, and top them with lids and rings, being sure not to tighten the rings all the way. Leave a bit of torque so air bubbles can escape. Process in a water bath for 10 minutes. Remove the jars with tongs and let them all cool on the counter. Once the jars are cool, make sure the seals are secure. Sealed jars may be stored in a cool dark cupboard for up to 1 year.

HOMEMADE APPLE CIDER VINEGAR

Apple cider vinegar is a soft, round vinegar that is slightly sweet. Perfect for dressing salads or using in pickles, this vinegar lacks the hard bite of traditional white vinegar. Apple cider vinegar is also a decent replacement for lemons when you don't have any around, and works well in a gravy or sauce.

It is fairly easy to make your own apple cider vinegar at home. You can use scraps from apples—the cores and skins make great starters. Use the scraps from apple pie or Green Apple Pectin (see p. 123) and you're off to a good start. Of course, you can use whole apples, as well; just be sure to choose ripe ones, as they have a higher sugar content than unripe apples. Choosing bruised apples, called seconds, at the farmers' market is an affordable option. This recipe forgoes any formal procuring of brewer's yeast, casks, and equipment, and sticks to using materials found in most homes. Use a large nonreactive pot for this project—a large stainless-steel pot or a deep earthenware pot work well.

With vinegar-making, oxygen needs to be present—in order for alcohol to turn to vinegar, it needs air. Oxygen on a liquid's surface will help bacteria in the process of converting alcohol to acetic acid, (the vinegar). You must watch for mold forming on the surface of your solution. Mold is an indication that the balance of acid to sugar is off; it generally will not form if the balance is right. In the event that mold presents itself on the apples' surface, skim it off and keep an eye on the jar. If mold develops again, toss the batch and start over—something may be off with the batch.

Makes 4 to 8 cups

Scraps from 10 apples (cores and peels),
   or 5 whole apples, finely chopped
¼ cup sugar

4 cups water
Cheesecloth

Put the apple pieces in a large pot. Dissolve the sugar in the water and pour over the apple scraps; they should be covered completely. If they are not, make another mixture of 4 cups water and ¼ cup sugar and add to the pot, but only enough to cover apples.

Cover the top of the pot with 4 layers of thick cheesecloth secured with kitchen twine, and set it in a warm spot in the kitchen. The interior of a cupboard works well, as does a countertop. (If you're making vinegar in summer, secure the cheesecloth tightly to prevent fruit flies from getting into the pot and laying eggs, which will spoil the batch.)

Leave the mixture for 1 week to macerate and ferment. The liquid may darken slightly and the apple mash will bubble—all signs of a good fermentation. After a week, strain out the apple mash from the liquid by setting it in a mesh strainer over a deep pot and allowing the mash to sit for 24 hours.

Return the apple liquid to the container with the mash, and cover it again with a thick layer of cheesecloth. Put the container in a warm spot and let it sit for 2 to 3 weeks, allowing the sugars to convert to vinegar. Stir or swirl the liquid every few days, to allow for air circulation and oxygen.

After 2 weeks, taste a spoonful of your vinegar for doneness. If the vinegar still tastes fruity and not acidic enough, let it sit for another week and taste again. After 3 weeks total, the liquid should be completely converted to apple cider vinegar.

To store apple cider vinegar, strain the liquid with a fine mesh sieve and pour it into clean, sterilized glass bottles. Store vinegar in a cool, dark place. Do not use homemade vinegar in canned goods, as acidity levels vary with each batch. Apple cider vinegar keeps indefinitely.

traditional apple butter

Makes about 5 half-pint jars

Apple butter is a traditional preserve—it's easy, and everyone loves it. Because apples are acidic enough to can safely in a water bath, you need only worry about the texture. Apples take time to cook down to the consistency of butter, so plan ahead for this project and block out an afternoon. Choosing apples is also an easy task—mix and match or stay true to one variety, but be sure to choose cooking apples that hold their flavor.

SUGGESTED VARIETIES: *I prefer Winesap, but plenty of other varieties work well. Try McIntosh, Spitzenburg, Rome, and Empire.*

2 cups water	1 lemon, juiced, halves reserved
4 cups apple cider	1 teaspoon ground cinnamon
4 pounds apples	½ teaspoon ground cloves
2 cups sugar	½ teaspoon freshly ground nutmeg

In a large stockpot, add the water and cider. Chop the apples into 1-inch pieces and add to the stockpot. (Yes, core, seeds, and all!) The liquid in the pot should just cover the fruit. If there is not enough liquid, add more cider or water to cover. Set over medium-high heat and bring to a boil. Reduce the heat to a gentle simmer and cook until all of the fruit is soft enough to mash with the back of a spoon. Working in batches, add the fruit to a blender (only half full at a time, as hot liquids expand) and puree. When all of the fruit is pureed, put it back into the stockpot, add the sugar, lemon juice and halves, and spices, and return to medium heat.

Cook the mixture over medium-low to medium heat, stirring every few minutes and taking care not to let it burn. If the fruit mixture is too hot and starts sticking to the bottom of the pot, lower the heat. After 1 hour of cooking, remove and discard the lemon halves. The butter is done when you can put a small spoonful on a plate and no liquid separates out to create a ring around the fruit butter. The cooking time can run anywhere from 1 to 2 hours.

Add the apple butter to clean, sterilized jars, leaving ¼ inch head space. Using a damp clean towel, wipe the rims of the jars, and top them with lids and rings, being sure not to tighten the rings all the way. Leave a bit of torque so air bubbles can escape. Process in a water bath for 10 minutes. Remove the jars with tongs and let them cool on the counter. Once the jars are cool, make sure the seals are secure. Sealed jars may be stored in a cool, dark cupboard for up to 1 year. You can also simply put the apple butter in jars and hold them in your fridge, where they will keep for several weeks.

rose hip & apple butter

Makes about 4 half-pint jars

Rose hips are the red buds that roses develop after their petals drop and can be foraged in late summer and through fall. These pretty buds are among my favorite wild foods to cook with, and add a delicate flavor to preserves. Rose hips are quite fibrous and take a fair amount of work to prepare for use in recipes, but it's worth the effort. Fruit butters can also take a long time to cook, so plan ahead for this kitchen project. This recipe starts with a rose hip puree and adds apples for a new twist on apple butter. Use on toast, as a fruit puree in plain yogurt, or as a base layer in tarts and pies.

SUGGESTED VARIETIES: *Apples that break down to a smooth puree do well here—opt for McIntosh, Rome, or Winesap.*

---

2 pounds rose hips, (8 to 10 cups)

5 to 7 medium apples (about 2 pounds), cut into 1-inch pieces

2 cups sugar

1 lemon, juiced, halves reserved

Cut the stems and ends from the rose hips and rinse. Add the rose hips to a large sauce-pan and just cover with water. Bring to a boil, then let simmer until soft, 45 minutes to 1 hour. Run the rose hips through a food mill, reserving the pulp. This will separate the skin, seeds, and hair from the rose hips and may take a few passes. The rose hip pulp is ready when you have a smooth puree, free of stringy hairs. Put the pulp in a fine-mesh strainer set over a bowl and push the puree through. This should catch any remaining hairs or seeds.

In a large saucepan, add the apples and enough water to just cover. Set over medium to medium-high heat and bring to a simmer. Cook until all of the fruit is soft enough that you can mash it with the back of a spoon.

Working in batches, put the apples in a blender (only half full at a time, as hot liquids expand) and puree. When all of the fruit is pureed, pour it into a fine-mesh strainer set over the saucepan. Push the puree through and back into the pot. Add the rose hip puree, sugar, lemon juice, and lemon halves to the apple puree. Return the mixture to medium-low to medium heat and cook, stirring every few minutes and taking care not to let it burn. If the fruit butter is too hot and starts sticking to the bottom of the pot, lower the heat.

The butter is done when you can put a small spoonful on a plate and no liquid separates out to create a ring around the fruit butter. The cooking time can run anywhere from 1 to 2 hours.

When the butter is cooked to a consistency of your liking, remove the lemon halves. Store the fruit butter in glass jars in the fridge, where it will keep for several weeks.

green apple pectin

Makes 2 pint jars

Pectin is found to varying degrees in fruit, but is particularly high in the skin, membranes, and seeds. Further, pectin is especially high in apples and citrus. Young, unripe fruits are particularly pectin-packed! The "green" in the recipe refers to this—unripe fruit. You can make your own pectin at home and add it to your low-pectin preserves (some berries, cherries) to help with the "set" of the jam. It's a great shortcut that you can do all by yourself—a very DIY project for the summer, as apple trees are just setting their fruit.

SUGGESTED VARIETIES: *Any undeveloped green apple picked from the tree before ripening.*

---

3 pounds unripe apples, stemmed and
   quartered

6 cups water

Juice of 1 small lemon

4½ cups sugar

Put the apple pieces in a large stockpot and cover with the water. Bring to a boil then reduce the heat, simmering for 30 minutes. Strain this apple mixture through a fine-mesh strainer, pressing lightly on the back of the fruit. Discard the solids and reserve the liquid.

Set a mesh strainer over a large bowl and line with 4 layers of moistened cheesecloth. Filter the apple liquid again through the cheesecloth, resulting in a mostly clear liquid.

Measure out 4¼ cups apple liquid and add to a saucepan with the lemon juice and sugar. Bring to a boil, skim the foam, and cook on high heat for about 10 minutes. You want a thick, syrupy or jammy set. Put the apple pectin in clean, sterilized jars leaving ¼ inch head space. Using a damp clean towel, wipe the rims of the jars, and top them with lids and rings. Process in a water bath for 10 minutes. Remove the jar with tongs and let it cool on the counter. Once it's cool, make sure the seal is secure. A sealed jar may be stored in a cool, dark cupboard for up to 1 year. You can also hold it in the fridge, where it will keep for several months.

apple pie filling

Makes 4 pint jars, enough for 2 pies

It is a good idea to buy apples in bulk when they're a new crop, fresh off the tree. It's both cheaper and assures the crispest, freshest apples. In order to make the most of the season, put up some apples that you can use later in the year. This simple recipe for apple pie filling guarantees you'll always have the best apples on hand for baking. Blanching them before you can them in a water bath also preserves their crispness, ensuring that they won't break down to mush when you bake them.

SUGGESTED VARIETIES: *Choose a firm and crisp apple, like Golden Delicious, Rome, or Cortland.*

---

6 pounds apples, cored and sliced

1 cup water

1 cup apple cider

1 cup sugar

¼ cup Green Apple Pectin (see p. 123), optional

¼ cup lemon juice

¼ teaspoon ground nutmeg

1 teaspoon ground cinnamon

¼ teaspoon ground cloves

Fill a large stockpot half full with water and bring to a boil. Drop in half of the sliced apples and cover, returning to a boil. Once the water boiling, 8 to 10 minutes, use a slotted spoon to strain out the apple slices. Add the slices directly to clean, sterilized pint jars, leaving some room. Repeat the process with the remaining apple slices, blanching until the water just boils before placing them in jars.

On a folded-over dish towel (for padding), strongly tap the bottom of the jar on the countertop, to help pack down the apples. If necessary, redistribute apples so each jar is full and has 1 inch head space.

In a medium saucepan, add the water, apple cider, sugar, Green Apple Pectin, if using, lemon juice, and spices; bring to a boil then reduce to a simmer. Simmer for 15 minutes, reducing slightly. Using a ladle or a liquid measuring cup for ease, pour the hot liquid over the jarred apples, leaving ½ inch head space. Gently tap the jars on the countertop to release any air bubbles. Using a damp clean towel, wipe the rims of the jars, and place the lids and rings on top, being sure not to tighten the rings all the way. Leave a bit of torque so air bubbles can escape. Process in a water bath for 20 minutes. Remove the jars with tongs and let them cool on the counter. Once they're cool, make sure the seals are secure. Sealed jars may be stored in a cool, dark cupboard for up to 1 year.

beet & apple relish

Makes about 2 pint jars

This relish adds a bit of spice to the table. It's a light and healthy appetizer that is perfect for starting the meal. Serve with grilled crostini or homemade tortilla chips. You can double the recipe and save extra for your pantry (can using the water-bath method) or make it in advance and store it in the fridge.

SUGGESTED VARIETIES: *A firm and flavorful apple is best in this relish. Try Granny Smith or Crispin.*

---

1 medium red onion, finely chopped
   (about 2 cups)

1½ cups water

½ cup apple cider vinegar

1 teaspoon salt

¼ cup sugar

1 teaspoon red pepper flakes

2 medium apples, cored and chopped

1 pound beets, trimmed, peeled, and cut
   into medium dice

In a large pot, add the onion, water, vinegar, salt, sugar, and red pepper flakes. Set over medium-high heat. Bring to a boil then reduce the heat to low, cooking for 5 minutes or until the onion is just cooked through and translucent. Add the apples and beets and cook for 20 to 30 minutes, just until the apples are cooked through but firm and the beets are just soft.

Transfer the relish to clean jars. Serve immediately or store in the fridge, where it will keep for 2 weeks.

korean apple relish

Makes 2 cups

Several years ago, a chef friend of mine served me a steamed Asian bun stuffed with barbecued pork belly and kimchi apples. The flavors were out of this world. I especially loved the spicy fermented taste of the kimchi in contrast to the sweet crispness of fresh apples. Here, we cheat a little by mixing fresh apples with kimchi brine, available at most grocery stores and Asian specialty markets. Choose a traditional Korean red kimchi for this recipe. Pair this relish with Fish Tacos (see p. 66) or serve alongside Apple & Red Lentil Steamed Dumplings (see p. 42) for a nutritious and flavor-packed meal.

SUGGESTED VARIETIES: *A sweet and tart apple that is super crisp works well here. Opt for Gala, Fuji, or Honeycrisp.*

---

3 medium apples, peeled, cored, and cut into ½-inch dice

1 carrot, peeled, cut into 2-inch lengths and thinly julienned

1 teaspoon sugar

¼ cup kimchi brine

In a medium bowl, add the apples, carrots, and sugar. Toss to combine. Pour in the kimchi brine and stir until all of the ingredients are well coated. Let sit for at least 30 minutes, but no more than 1 hour, before serving. The apples will only hold their shape for a few hours, so do not make this dish too far ahead.

APPLE STAMPS

Fruit stamping is an easy and rewarding project that won't
break the bank and is engaging to children of all ages. (And adults!)
Kids can work independently, applying paint to the apples and stamping on their
own. Apples are sliced width-wise exposing the natural star shape of the core,
and then brushed with a thin layer of paint. These homemade stamps can then be
used to decorate plain white flour sacks, or create kid-made holiday cards or simple
canvas totes for gift giving. Red Delicious apples have beautiful shapes that are
excellent for stamping. It is also worth the effort to source small backyard apples,
like crab apples—their diminutive size is a nice balance to the larger Red Delicious.

Various colors of fabric paint

3 Red Delicious apples

1 paintbrush or sponge

Plain canvas tote bags, flour sacks, or
blank note cards

Set out as many small plates as you have colors of fabric paint. Pool a shallow
amount of paint in the center of each plate.

To prepare the apples, cut them in half across the center, width-wise. Press the
apple flesh into a layer of paper towel, working to absorb excess moisture before
stamping.

Press an apple, cut-side down, into the fabric paint. Use a paintbrush to brush off
any extra paint. You are looking for a thin layer of paint, so that it doesn't bleed out
and lose the apple shape.

Press the painted apple half into the material you are working with. Be sure to have
kids hold the apple half down firmly with even pressure in order to capture the
entire shape of the apple.

Continue working in this fashion until each project is complete, reapplying fabric
paint and brushing off after each stamp. Set projects aside to dry completely before
handling.

star-anise-pickled apple slices

Makes 1 cup

In fall when apples are just coming in, we tend to cook more homey foods—roasts and heavy soups. Pickles are the perfect counterpoint to these deep flavors. For softer produce, like apples, a quick pickle works best, so the apples are not sitting in brine and breaking down to mush. Here, the pickling liquid is heated only slightly and the apples are left to brine in the fridge. These pickled apples are a perfect side dish for roasted or barbecued pork but will also go well with any braised meat or on a sandwich. This recipe makes a small portion, because apples will only keep for a day before they start to lose their crispness and really break down.

SUGGESTED VARIETIES: *A firm and flavorful apple is best in pickles. Try Granny Smith or Crispin.*

1½ cups apple cider vinegar

2 tablespoons sugar

One 3-inch piece fresh gingerroot, peeled and cut into coins

2 whole star anise

5 whole cloves

1 teaspoon whole peppercorns

Pinch of salt

2 medium apples, peeled and cored

In a medium saucepan, heat the apple cider vinegar, sugar, ginger, star anise, cloves, peppercorns, and salt over medium heat until all of the sugar has dissolved. Remove the pan from the heat and set aside until just warm. You should be able to hold your finger in the vinegar for any amount of time without it burning or feeling hot.

While the brine is cooling slightly, cut the apples into ¼-inch slices and put in a non-reactive bowl, such as a glass mixing bowl. When the brine is cooled to warm, pour it over the apples and put the bowl in the fridge. The apples are done when the brine has cooled completely and the apples are pickled but still crisp.

apple pear salsa with cilantro

Makes 1 cup

This salsa is a refreshing side to winter dishes of any kind. The heat from the jalapeño cuts through roasted meats to add a fresh note to meals. This salsa also works well as an accompaniment to Fish Tacos (see p. 66) or Hard-Cider-Braised Short Ribs (see p. 78). Pears break down quickly and do not hold well, so the recipe is intentionally a small portion—enough for just one meal.

SUGGESTED VARIETIES: *Fresh-eating apples are best in salsas. Try Cameo, Honeycrisp, or Crimson Delight.*

---

1 medium apple, cored and cut into small dice

1 medium pear, cored and cut into small dice

1 cup chopped fresh cilantro (about ⅓ bunch)

1 teaspoon salt

¼ teaspoon freshly ground pepper

2 tablespoons finely chopped seeded jalapeño

Juice from 1 lime

In a medium bowl, stir all of the ingredients together until well blended. Serve immediately.

resources

There are a vast many apple resources for growers and farmers across the United States. While you're best off seeking out a local farmers' market in your area, the following are some associations that will have good regional representation. These associations are mostly used to support the business of selling apples, but they provide good references lists for your local apple farmers. You will also find some readings for anyone wanting to dig a bit deeper.

FARMERS' MARKETS
search.ams.usda.gov/farmersmarkets
A list of national farmers' markets. Support your local food producers and small family farms!

RENEWING AMERICA'S FOOD TRADITIONS
www.raflalliance.org
Save our seeds! Seeds are a precious resource that should be saved— find out more here.

APPLE GROWERS' ASSOCIATIONS
New England Apple Association
www.newenglandapples.org

North Carolina Apple Growers association
www.ncapplegrowers.com

NY Apple Association
www.nytapplecountry.com

Ohio Apples
www.ohioapples.com

Michigan Apple Committee
www.michiganapples.com

Minnesota Apple Growers Association
www.minnesotaapple.org

Washington State Apple Commission
www.bestapples.com

Tree Fruit Research & Extension Center–Washington State University
www.tfrec.wsu.edu

Great Lakes Cider & Perry Association
www.greatlakescider.com

Northwest Cider Association
www.nwcider.com

Forgotten Fruits Manual & Manifesto by Gary Paul Nabhan
www.slowfoodusa.org/images/ark_products/applebklet_web-3-11.pdf

This report is one of several mutually reinforcing efforts catalyzed by the Renewing America's Food Traditions (RAFT) Alliance to celebrate both heirloom apples and the rich American apple culture that surrounds them.

CIDER MAKERS AND FRUIT NURSERIES
Alma Orchards
almarorchards.com
Cider and organic apples in the Midwest.

Crane Orchards
craneorchards.com
U-pick nursery in Michigan.

New England Apples
www.newenglandapples.org
A resource for nurseries, cider houses, u- picks, and general education about growing apples.

Johnson Nursery, Inc.
1352 Big Creek Rd., Ellijay, GA 30536
"Hardy Fruit trees for homeowners" in the Southeast.

Raintree Nursery
www.raintreenursery.com
Fruit trees, including dwarf, conical, and espalier apples for the Pacific Northwest growing conditions and more.

Rocky Mountain Cider Association
www.rmcider.org
Apple and pear cider makers in the Mountain West.

Seedling Fruit
www.seedlingfruit.com
Apple cider purveyors in the Midwest.

index

acknowledgments

Putting a book together is always a fantastic project to be involved with, but is also a labor of love. I owe a massive thank you to main-laborer, Dana Youlin at becker&mayer, for bringing this project to me, being a great editor and willing recipe tester, and for offering her critique and guidance along the way. She deserves a medal in patience. Another huge thanks to the rest of the crew at becker&mayer; especially Kara Stokes for her photo shoot enthusiasm and help, and Rosebud Eustace for her keen eye and amazing design skills on this book. Isn't it gorgeous? Along with this crew, big thanks to the posse over at St. Martin's Griffin for allowing me to work on this project with them. I so appreciate it!

This book would not look half as lovely if not for the stunning photography from Oliva Brent. It was an honor and pleasure to work with this young, budding food photographer, along with her assistant, Shannon Oslick. Their dedication to getting the perfect shot is unparalleled and these PYTs definitely taught this old dog a new trick or two. Thank you!

I would also like to thank my brother and sister for helping with this book! My brother Seth Pennington, maker of the requisite Thanksgiving apple pie, shared his stellar recipe with me and I used it as a jumping off point for the Traditional Pie. My sister, Stacy Bartholomew, is a patient and humorous mother of five children under the age of 11 and offered her ideas and wisdom for all of the kids projects in the book, as well as the stuffed French toast recipe. Love you both! A final thanks to my favorite consort, Kenneth Dundas for tasting 87 million caramel apple tarts even when I burned the sugar, always offering his thoughtful opinions on my projects and for his unending support and cheerleading.

about the photographer

Olivia Brent is a Pacific Northwest–based food photographer who fell in love with photography at an early age. She now brings that passion to each shoot, working to capture a sense of personality and place with each dish. Her work has led her to frequently collaborate with local companies, publications, and chefs, and can be explored further at www.oliviabrentphotography.com.

about the author

Food writer, organic gardener, and cook Amy Pennington is the creator/owner of GoGo Green Garden, an edible gardening business that builds, plants, and tends edible gardens for city folk in their backyards. She is the author of *Urban Pantry: Tips & Recipes for a Thrifty, Sustainable & Seasonal Kitchen* and *Apartment Gardening: Plants, Projects, and Recipes for Growing Food in Your Urban Home. Fresh Pantry*, her newest project, is a monthly e-book series, launched in January 2013. She is a contributing writer to *Edible Seattle*, as well as Crosscut.com, Food52. com, and *Sip Northwest Magazine*. Amy has been featured on Whole Living Martha Stewart Sirius Radio, GOOP, *Bon Appetit*, Apartment Therapy, the *New York Times T* Magazine blog, and the *Wall Street Journal*. She lives in Seattle.
Visit www.amy-pennington.com to learn more.

Book Design: Rosebud Eustace
Editor: Dana Youlin
Photo Editor: Kara Stokes

Library of Congress Cataloging-in-Publication Date available upon request.

ISBN: 978-1-250-03906-4

St. Martin's Griffin books may be purchased for educational, business, or promotional use. For information on bulk purchases, please contact Macmillan Corporate and Premium Sales Department at 1-800-221-7945 extension 5442 or write specialmarkets@macmillan.com.

First Edition: September 2013

10 9 8 7 6 5 4 3 2 1

Design element throughout: Apple cultivar, Washington, Malus domestica © Florilegius / The Natural History Museum, London; Apple, Mr. Gladstone variety, Malus domestica © Florilegius / The Natural History Museum, London; Werder's Golden Reinette apple, Malus domestica © Florilegius / The Natural History Museum, London Pyrus sp., apple (The Ribstone Pippin apple) © The Natural History Museum, London; Pyrus sp., apple (Fearn's Pippin apple) © The Natural History Museum, London.

Apples: From Farm to Table *is produced by becker&mayer!, Bellevue, Washington.*
www.beckermayer.com